QUICK & EASY
DECORATING

EDITORIAL
Craft Editor: Tonia Todman
Managing Editor: Judy Poulos
Editorial Coordinator: Margaret Kelly
Craft Assistants: Martina Oprey; Susie
Ting; Sally Pereira; Rosa Alonso

UK EDITOR: Georgina Evans

PRODUCTION
Tara Barrett
Chris Hatcher

ILLUSTRATIONS
Margie Mulray

PHOTOGRAPHY
Harm Mol

COVER DESIGN
Frank Pithers

DESIGN AND PRODUCTION
MANAGER
Nadia Sbisa

PUBLISHER
Philippa Sandall

Published by J.B. Fairfax Press
Pty Ltd
80-82 McLachlan Avenue
Rushcutters Bay NSW Australia 2011
© J.B. Fairfax Press Pty Ltd 1991

Family Circle is a registered trademark of
IPC Magazines Ltd
Published by J. B. Fairfax Press Pty Ltd by
arrangement with IPC Magazines Ltd

QUICK AND EASY DECORATING
ISBN 1 86343 017 2

Formatted by J.B. Fairfax Press Pty Ltd
Output by Adtype, Sydney
Printed by Toppan Printing Co, Hong Kong

Distributed in the UK by
J.B. Fairfax Press Ltd
9 Trinity Centre, Park Farm Estate
Wellingborough, Northants UK
Tel: (0933) 402330
Fax: (0933) 402234

Contents

Introduction

*The secret of successful home decorating is to combine careful planning and a sensible budget with your own creative flair and energy. If you research the project thoroughly, you'll wind up having a lot of fun, learn new skills, save money **and** increase the value of your home. On top of all that, there's the satisfaction of knowing you did it yourself!*

What are your needs?

❏ Is this your first nest? Does it look a bit tired and in need of some tender loving care?

❏ Have you lived there for many years? Do you feel it's time for a change now that the children are nearly off your hands and you can indulge your own tastes at long last?

❏ Are you renting an apartment, and limited in the amount of redecoration you can attempt, but want to update with new curtains and bright accessories?

A business couple who spend little time in their tiny city apartment have different needs to young parents with two children and a dog. Students need more bookshelves and study space than a single parent with a couple of active toddlers in tow.

Have a good look at what you can live with for a little bit longer and what just has to go right now. Fake it, if you can, with budget-conscious decorative paint techniques for walls, floors and furniture (see pages 26, 38, 46). 'Faux' decorating is all the rage but it has to look great to avoid ending up with a tawdry result, so prepare the surfaces carefully and read the instructions.

A good scrub with sugar soap works wonders on tired walls and ceilings. It could enable you to postpone a full paint job in the bathroom, allowing you to spend a little more on new curtains or a beautifully framed print for the living room.

Make sure your planned renovations are user-friendly and will actually improve your quality of life. If you want to start a family next year, don't choose a plush upholstery fabric – it simply isn't practical.

If you are an apartment dweller or rent your home, consider the advantages of portable decorating projects, such as cushions, loose covers and accessories. Wonderful effects can be achieved with a little ingenuity – and you can take them with you when you move!

Sit down with the family and discuss everyone's needs. Write them down in a sturdy notebook – used wisely, this will become your 'bible' and you'll carry it everywhere. Add a pen, a good tape measure and a colour card and you are ready to begin exploring the possibilities. A camera for taking pictures from different angles in the home may prove useful.

Laura Ashley (Australia) Pty Limited

Saving money makes sense. Always ask if you can get a price reduction for cash and shop around for the best price and service. Comparison shopping may take a little time but can save you lots of money. How can you be sure you've really discovered a bargain if you don't know the usual price? Take advantage of genuine sales, always buy the best product and most comprehensive service you can afford and do it right! A good carpet laid over a quality underlay is a better buy than a 'bargain' that doesn't wear well. You may have to wait a little longer for something special or do the work in stages, but it's worth the trouble to get what you really want. In the meantime, we can show you how to make beautiful alternatives that won't break the bank.

Laura Ashley (Australia) Pty Limited

Left and below: Remember always decorate to suit your lifestyle and your budget

What can you afford?

Working to a budget is vital. Obviously you will have certain financial commitments that must take priority over new curtains or a pot of paint, whether you're paying rent or paying off a mortgage. Decide how much cash you can spare now and, say, over the next year...or will you need to borrow money – and from whom? How does borrowing fit into your long term plans for holidays, new clothes, the children's education? Even if your decorating project won't cost much, decide how much you can afford and then stick to your budget! Interest on borrowings can be a trap. That new chair you buy in the sale won't be a bargain if you buy it on credit and pay interest.

Nairn Floors

4

Make your plans

Having a plan is essential to the success of any home decorating exercise, no matter how big or small. A plan will help you to save money, avoiding those impulse buys (that you regret the next day), and feel satisfied with the end results. After all, you'll have to live with them – perhaps for a long time.

This is when you really need your 'bible'.

❑ Measure everything – walls to estimate paint quantities, wall-paper and friezes; windows for tracks, rods and curtain fabric; floors for carpets and tiles; doors for new handles; furniture and cupboards…the lot!

❑ Take photographs of rooms and features you want to change.

❑ Making a floor plan is essential and it's easy if you use graph paper to scale down room sizes. Don't forget to include windows and doors, steps, built-in cup-boards, electrical and plumbing fittings room by room. Now you can cut out paper models of all your existing furniture to move around the paper plan, instead of dragging heavy furniture around the room.

Store the measurements, photographs and room plan in envelopes pasted inside the cover of your 'bible' so that you'll have them with you all the time. If you know the floor size of all your rooms, you'll be able to snap up a bargain when you see a carpet or tile sale.

Calling in a professional

Paying a professional tradesman is unavoidable in some cases. Local regulations may demand that electrical, plumbing or building work is carried out by

accredited tradespeople who have the training, the tools and the authority to tackle some jobs which amateurs should never attempt. Check with your local authority. You may need to consult an expert about the soundness of walls and floors before you start redecorating.

Get it in writing

This is the golden rule whenever you commission work. A written quote should include all costs and details of all materials to be used (quality and quantity); it should stipulate a completion date and must be written in clear language. Don't accept the quote unless you can understand it and

accept everything in it. Ask for proof of the contractor's licence, or other accreditation. Satisfy yourself that you are adequately protected by his or her insurance, covering damage to your prop-erty and injury to anyone em-ployed by the contractor to do your job.

Do you need an interior designer?

Paying for advice from an interior designer is a sound investment if you can afford it. It costs nothing to ask for an 'advisory price' and scale of fees. Don't be embar-rassed to say you have a budget – reputable designers will be delighted to find a client who

Country Form

Left: Natural timbers are the perfect choice for your kitchen. Properly prepared and sealed, they are easy to care for and pleasant to live with for many years
Below right: Putting together a new decorating scheme can be a great challenge and lots of fun! For a bright contemporary look, use lots of high tech, shiny chrome and strong colours

brushing up old ones. We'll help you with tips on choosing fabric and displaying your accessories; we'll show you clever ways with paint and paper but you can also take classes in colour, lighting, painting techniques, tile-laying. You name it, somebody's teaching it! Adult education groups, technical schools, manufacturers, department stores and building information centres are all valuable sources of free or moderately priced tuition. Avoid expensive correspondence courses – you really need the hands-on experience. Take a course in household repairs and restoration, a sound investment which will teach you how to save money by doing your own repairs. Remember, knowing the

knows how much he or she wants to spend. If you're not sure how to find a designer, refer to the local telephone directory. There may be a national association, such as The Interior Decorators' and Designers' Association, who will supply a list of their members. Or try chatting to staff at your favourite soft furnishing supplier. Some department stores offer a 'free' decorating service to their customers. There is no charge if you subsequently place an order, otherwise a nominal fee applies. Ask for details before committing yourself to avoid misunderstandings and unexpected costs.

Plan your schedule

Good timing can help things run smoothly and can ease the financial burden of the work. Will redecorating disrupt your household, and how long will your routine be affected? An asthmatic child may need to spend a couple of days with friends while old

carpet is ripped up. Before you commission tradespeople to work for you, coordinate the job to be done – each stage has to be completed in the right sequence or you may face a lot of extra costs and many frustrating delays.

It's very important to allow sufficient time to do a good job – don't try to rush it. If you can't quite afford the exact curtains you want, maybe you could manage with lining fabric for a while? Thorough research and the right tools won't guarantee satisfactory results but a comprehensive schedule which gives you plenty of time for preparation, application and finishing will help a great deal. If you think the job is too big to tackle on your own, throw a 'working party'. You supply the materials and all the food and drinks (and the work!) and ask family and friends to come over and lend a hand in return for a few laughs and supper.

Learning can be fun, whether you're acquiring new skills or

IKEA

'nuts and bolts' of a job helps you tell the difference between a fair quote and a rip-off.

It's important to be able to recognise a bargain when you see one. But look carefully – will that old dresser respond to restorative techniques or would you be wasting your money buying a piece of junk?

Decorating with colour

Choosing the right colour is as important when decorating your house as it is when choosing your clothes – you live in both of them! Colour is affected by lighting (particularly artificial lights) and where you use it. You can make rooms seem bigger, smaller, taller, wider or even

create a special mood with the right colours.

Whenever you select furnishings or paint, take a sample home so that you can judge the colour in the place and lighting conditions you have planned for it. Give yourself two or three options to choose from in case your first choice isn't available.

Collecting samples

Collecting samples will become a passion once you start planning. Fabric swatches, scraps of wallpaper and friezes, paint cards, colour wheels and lighting brochures will burst from your 'bible'. Your diary will be filled with appointments to view carpets, curtains, blinds and furnishings at home (check that this service is obligation-free). Seeing them at home is the most efficient way to choose colours and textures for large areas – and cuts your time and fuel costs, too!

Trial and error

Before starting a big project, try out your ideas on a small scale. Buy sample-sized pots of paint and try them on the wall, remembering that colours can change. For instance, pastels paint up three or four times more intensely than they appear on a colour card.

All laminated surfaces can be painted – the trick is to find the right 'key' or surface preparation to accept the paint. Treat a small, unobtrusive section first to test your 'key' before embarking on the entire job.

Don't be deterred by little disappointments and mistakes. They're all learning experiences that can help you avoid costly problems when you tackle the

real thing. Keep a record of tests and results, successes and failures in your 'bible' for future reference. Note what went wrong and if you were able to correct it – a photograph might help, too. Living with your new look is the best part. Looking at a beautiful finish and knowing you did it yourself is a very satisfying experience.

Now you have an endless source of suggestions for fellow do-it-yourself fans and, if you were clever enough to take 'before' and 'after' photos for your 'bible', you will have the best brag book in town!

So off you go – just remember the basic principles of good planning, sensible budgeting and learning from your mistakes. When you've finished the first project, start another one. We have lots of suggestions for you and practical, easy to follow instructions. Good luck!

HINT
Create files of 'how-to' hints from magazines and newspapers that publish regular decorating features. Cut out and file anything you feel may be useful in the future. You'll gradually get to know which writers or magazines are on your wavelength, with ideas to suit your budget, so watch out for them.

Windows
with style

*B*righten a dull room in a flash
with new curtains or practical,
sophisticated fabric blinds. Decide
which look best suits your window,
the rest of your decor and lifestyle.
If you like the softness of gathered
and ruffled material, combined with
the decorating possibilities of today's
wonderful fabric prints, then curtains
are more your style. If you prefer the
clean lines and monochromatic feel
of the city apartment, then Roman
blinds are just right for you.

Simple Curtains

Making your own curtains is not at all difficult and very economical.

Before You Begin

❑ You will need to measure the window you wish to cover with curtains.

❑ To calculate your length, measure from the top of the curtain track to the floor or window-sill or, in the case of a curtain pole and rings, measure from the eye hook at the bottom of the rings to the floor. Allow an extra 20 cm in total for turning under at the top and bottom. Curtains will finish approximately 5 cm above the top of the track or eye hook of the ring.

❑ The width measurement will depend on the thickness of your fabric. For very sheer fabrics you will need up to 3 times the length of the curtain track. For medium-weight fabrics you will need $2^1/_2$ times the length of the track while twice the track length is acceptable for heavier fabrics.

❑ Sheer fabrics are traditionally not lined. Medium-weight fabrics can benefit from lining, as lined curtains become good insulators and are most effective in controlling light. Try to make your curtain linings the same colour on all your windows, otherwise the exterior view could become a patchwork of multi-coloured linings. You will need the same width of lining as for your main fabric. Lining fabrics are often very wide, so you may need to buy less fabric than for your main fabric.

❑ Consult your curtain accessory shop about the most appropriate heading tape for your fabric. Which one you choose will depend on the type of track or pole you have installed, the weight of your fabric and the effect you want – normally standard gathered tape, pencil pleat or triple pleat (also called pinch pleat). Our curtains have a thick wooden rod over which wooden rings are threaded. These have a small ring at the bottom through which the heading tape hook is inserted. You will need a length of heading tape equal to the total width of your curtain plus 10 cm for side hems and ease. For example, if you use four drops of 115 cm wide fabric you will need 4.70 m of tape.

Top: The fabric-covered pole and painted-to-match curtain rings
Above: The back of the curtain showing the pleating tape and the way in which it is pleated using the special hooks available where you buy the tape
Above right: The simple curtain with pleated heading, fabric-covered curtain pole and fittings painted to match the fabric

MATERIALS

☐ sufficient main fabric for curtain (see *Before You Begin*)
☐ sufficient lining fabric (see *Before You Begin*)
☐ sufficient heading tape (see *Before You Begin*)
☐ sufficient rings or hooks for your track or pole
☐ matching sewing threads

METHOD

See the Pull Out Pattern Sheet at the back of the book for the window measurement diagram.

1 Cut your main fabric and lining into the lengths you have calculated in *Before You Begin*.

2 Stitch main fabric lengths together down the long sides until you have the complete curtain width. Do this for lining lengths as well. Turn under 1 cm on the outside edges of main fabric piece then turn under another 5 cm. Baste. Stitch along inner fold. Do this for lining piece as well, folding under 7 cm at sides.

3 Press both pieces. Place them together with wrong sides facing so that 1 cm of main fabric extends beyond the lining on both sides, and top and bottom raw edges are even. Turn over 3 cm of both curtain and lining *together* at top. Press and pin in place.

4 If using pencil pleating tape, unravel the draw cords of the first 5 cm of the tape. For triple pleating tape, such as

6 Turn up curtain hem. Pin and baste. Turn up the lining hem to sit 2 cm shorter than the curtain. Remove the curtain from the track. Stitch both hems. Press to finish.

Fabric-covered pole

MATERIALS

- ☐ wooden curtain pole
- ☐ sufficient wooden curtain rings
- ☐ a pair of finials (end stoppers)
- ☐ sufficient fabric to cover (see *Before You Begin*)
- ☐ fabric or craft glue

METHOD

1 Cut a rectangular piece of fabric the length of the pole and the width of the circumference of the pole plus 3 cm for overlap.

2 If not using the selvage of the fabric, finish one long edge of the fabric by folding under 6 mm. Wrap the fabric around the pole with the folded edge covering the raw edge. Glue into place.

3 Finials can also be covered by using fabric cut on the bias, pleating out the fullness and cutting out these small pleats so that fabric lies flat with no gaps. The pattern will not match on these pieces, but it does not seem to matter! If you are worried by the possibility of gaps, you can paint the finials the same colour as the background colour of the fabric before you begin covering the pole.

4 You can cover all the rings with fabric too. Or you can simply paint them in a colour to complement your fabric.

Below: Sometimes all you need is a little imagination! You can make this elegant, draped pelmet simply by trimming a suitable length of fabric and draping it over your curtain track or pole as shown here. Take care that the right side of your fabric is always the one showing

ours, turn in raw end of tape so that you have a hook channel just in from the edge of the curtain. Pin the upper edge of the tape to the curtain 1.5 cm down from the top. Stitch down all edges of the tape. If you are using pencil pleating tape, draw up the cords to gather the curtain and insert the hooks into the channels. If you are using triple pleating tape, insert the pronged hooks according to the manufacturer's instructions. This will give the pleated effect.

5 Hang the curtain and leave it to hang for twenty-four hours to allow the fabric to ease and 'drop'. After twenty-four hours, and while the curtains are still hanging, make the connecting 'ties' between the side edges of the curtain and lining .

Laura Ashley (Australia) Pty Limited

Down to DETAIL

Cafe Curtains

This simple method of window dressing will afford privacy and at the same time allow plenty of light to enter the room. Cafe curtains can be casual or formal, soft and feminine or dramatically contemporary, depending on the fabric you choose. Plain fabrics can be stencilled, appliqued or braid-trimmed.

are two identical curtains which part in the middle.

❏ Remember to measure from the top of the rods when calculating fabric lengths for both curtains. Add a hem and casing allowance to each fabric drop (i.e. length of fabric) – 20 cm for the upper curtain and 26 cm for the lower curtain. For example, assuming that your upper curtain is to finish 30 cm from the top of the rod and your lower curtain is to finish 50 cm from the top of the lower rod, you will need to cut your upper curtain into drops of 50 cm, and your lower curtain into drops of 76 cm.

❏ Generally, you will find each curtain requires a total fabric width of 2¼ times the length of the rod. If you are using a sheer fabric, or lace, you may wish to increase this to 2½ times or even 3 times the length of the rod. For example, if your rod is 1 m long, you will need to seam together enough fabric drops to produce a total width of 2.25 m plus side and centre turn under allowances.

❏ To calculate fabric quantities for our curtains on your window follow the simple formulas below.
For the upper curtain the total length of the drops required to make up the required width, allowing 10 cm in total for side hems plus 20 cm per drop for casing and hem.
For the lower curtain the total length of the drops required to make up the required width, allowing 20 cm in total for side and centre hems plus 26 cm per drop for casing loops and hem.

MATERIALS
☐ sufficient fabric for upper and lower curtains (see *Before You Begin*)
☐ matching sewing thread
☐ strong handsewing needle
☐ curtain pole, brackets and rings

METHOD
For the upper curtain:

1 Join short ends of fabric drops to create the total width. Turn in 1 cm on the side edges, then turn another 4 cm and press. Stitch along the inner fold.

2 Turn over 1 cm on upper edge, then turn another 8 cm and press. Stitch along the inner fold. Stitch again 4 cm from previous stitching, creating the rod casing. The fabric above the casing will form a frill when the rod is inserted.

HINT
When choosing fabrics for your Cafe Curtains note that the broad stripe shown emphasises the hanging loops beautifully, but don't overlook trimming plain fabrics with broad bands of braid, strips of contrast fabric or cotton lace. Fabrics with printed borders of all descriptions can be effective too, especially when the border is used vertically at the centre opening of the lower curtain or repeated across both the top and bottom curtains.

3 Turn up 1 cm on the lower edge, then turn another 4 cm and press. Stitch along the first fold. Press.

For the lower curtains:
See the Pull Out Pattern Sheet at the back of the book for the template for the cut out.

1 The instructions are for one curtain. Make two the same. Join fabric drops, if necessary, to create the required width for the lower curtain. Turn in 1 cm on one side of curtain, then turn another 4 cm and press. Stitch along the first fold.

2 Fold 1 cm over to the wrong side on the top edge and press. Fold over another 25 cm on the top edge so that right sides are facing. Press.

3 Cut a cardboard template from the shape on the pattern sheet. Check that this is long enough to loop over your curtain pole, and adjust its size if necessary. Place the template at the top edge, 8 cm in from the hemmed side edge of the curtain. Mark the shapes across the curtain, about 10 cm apart or to suit your fabric pattern. Mark where you will place the final scallop, leaving 8 cm as on the other end and allowing for the side hem. Cut off any excess fabric.

4 Open out the marked top of the curtain. Turn in 1 cm along the side edge, then turn another 4 cm and press. Stitch along first crease. Fold the top of the curtain again. Stitch around the marked shapes and cut out. Trim and clip into curves for ease. Turn loops to the right side and press. At the back, bring the top of the loop to the base of the loop. Stitch through all thicknesses.

5 Thread the pole through the loops to hang the curtain.

6 If you wish to cover the curtain pole with matching fabric, this is quite easy to do. You can use your curtain fabric or you can choose a contrasting one. See the instructions on page 11 for how to cover your curtain pole.

Top left: The upper curtain showing the rod casing and frill
Centre left: The lower curtain showing the rod threaded through the loops

Festoon or Cloud Blinds

For a romantic look, nothing beats festoon blinds. The fabric you choose will set the style for your blind, from the soft and feminine look of sheer lace to the dramatic elegance of silk brocade. These are in simple homespun cotton for a contemporary feel.

Before You Begin

❑ To calculate your fabric requirements, measure the width and length of your window. You will need a piece of fabric twice this length by twice this width. If you need to join fabric to achieve this width, do so with small flat seams.

MATERIALS

For each blind:
- ☐ fabric (see *Before You Begin*)
- ☐ pencil pleating tape, twice the width of your window
- ☐ ring tape, four times your blind length plus 24 cm
- ☐ one cleat for fastening blind cords
- ☐ metal rod or dowelling for holding lower

edge, 1 cm in diameter to measure 2.5 cm shorter than the width of the window.
- ☐ eyelet screws – one for each length of ring tape plus one
- ☐ curtain track of your choice
- ☐ sufficient hooks for fastening blind to track

METHOD

See the Pull Out Pattern Sheet at the back of the book for the cord threading diagram.

1 Turn in 2.5 cm on the top and sides of fabric piece (or joined pieces). Press.

2 Unravel the draw cords of the first 5 cm of the pencil pleating tape. Pin the upper edge of the tape to the top of your blind fabric, 1.5 cm from the edge. Stitch down all edges of the tape, stitching the top hem as you go. Do not draw up the cords.

3 Turn under 1 cm on the lower edge and then turn another 4 cm. Press. Stitch bottom hem.

4 Stitch ring tape down side hems (fixing hems in place at the same time), and at two equally-spaced points across the blind from top to bottom hems. Leave an extra 6 cm of tape at the bottom of each length.

5 Loop this tape back on itself so that the end is just above the hem. Stitch. These loops are to hold the bottom rod.

6 Gather pencil pleating cord, until the blind gathers to the width of the track.

7 Attach eyelets to the window frame, just below the track, to correspond with the top of each strip of ring tape and another, just below one curtain track bracket, through which you will thread blind cords.

8 Cut a cord for each strip of tape, long enough to reach from the bottom rod, up the blind, through the eyelets, across the top and down to the side where the extra eyelet is, leaving sufficient length for knotting them together below the eyelet.

9 Thread the cords up from the bottom, tying the three bottom rings together as you go to form a permanent blousing effect. Attach the blind to the curtain track with the hooks. Insert the rod through the tape loops at the lower edge of the blind.

Roman Blinds

For a more tailored window treatment, consider these Roman blinds.

Before You Begin

❑ Roman blinds are traditionally fitted inside the window frame. They retain one or two pleats even when let down. Take this into account when measuring.

❑ To calculate your fabric requirements: You will need the desired width of the blind plus 10 cm for hems x the desired length of the blind plus 30 cm at the top for turning plus 12 cm for each timber lath plus 13 cm for the lower hem and lath pocket.

❑ Decide how many lath pockets you want to have by making a paper pattern of the blind. Fold in the 30 cm at the top and the 5 cm at the lower edge and then crease in the lath pockets. Do this until you are happy with the number and spacing of your laths – generally six or eight.

❑ Fabrics with strong patterns or ones that do not adequately screen the light, may need to be lined. Cut the lining fabric the same size as the main fabric. Baste the two pieces together, with wrong sides facing, and from here on treat them as a single layer, following the instructions below. Remember to choose a lining fabric in keeping with that on the other windows so your house is as attractive from the outside as it is inside.

MATERIALS

- ❑ sufficient fabric and lining (optional) (see *Before You Begin*)
- ❑ 5 cm wide contrast fabric strip or braid x four times the length of the blind, before stitching the pockets
- ❑ matching sewing thread
- ❑ sufficient 5 cm wide timber laths, as wide as the finished width of the blind (see *Before You Begin*)
- ❑ a mounting board the width of your window, 2 cm thick and 7 cm deep.
- ❑ one pair metal 'L' brackets
- ❑ tacks or a staple gun
- ❑ nylon cord about 6 mm thick for raising and lowering the blind
- ❑ sufficient eye hooks to have two for each lath, two on the mounting board and one more at one end of the mounting board
- ❑ one metal cleat for tying off the cords

METHOD

See the Pull Out Pattern Sheet at the back of the book for the construction diagram.

1 Turn 1 cm on both sides of the blind fabric piece to the right side. Press. Turn in 1 cm on long sides of contrast fabric strips. Press. Pin one strip to each edge of the blind, covering the pressed raw edge and having the pressed edges of the strip and blind matching. Stitch both long edges of the contrast strip to the blind. Stitch the other two strips one-third of the way in from the sides. Turn 1 cm on the upper and lower edges to the wrong side. Press. On the lower edge turn under 6 cm and stitch down, forming the last lath pocket.

2 Mark each lath pocket with two lines 12 cm apart. On the outside of the fabric, bring these two lines together. Pin and baste along marked lines. Stitch, forming the lath pockets. Carefully stitch the folded edge of each lath pocket down onto the blind. Insert the laths.

3 On the wrong side of the blind, screw an eye hook through the fabric into each lath about a quarter of the way in from the sides. Make sure that all your hooks run down the blind in a straight line.

4 Attach your mounting board to the wall above the window frame with metal 'L' brackets.

5 Tack or staple the top edge of the fabric to the top of the mounting board, close to the back (wall) edge so that the fabric covers the top of the board and hangs down the front of it, concealing the board altogether. Screw two eye hooks into the underside of the mounting board, each one in line with a row of eye hooks on the blind. Screw another eye hook into one end of the underside of the mounting board on the same side as you will mount the cleat for holding the cords on the window frame.

6 Secure a cord at the lowest eye hook on each side of the blind. Thread the cords up the row of eye hooks on the blind, including those on the mounting board, so that both cords emerge at the extra eye hook on one side of the mounting board. Knot the cords together below the level of the cleat.

Tracks and Rods

Your choice of curtain rods, poles or tracks will be based on the shape and function of your window, the effect you want to create – and your budget. If you live in rented accommodation, you should opt for rods or poles which are usually less expensive, easier to install and highly portable. Special extendable poles allow you to change the length to suit different windows – another plus for rent-payers!

Unless curtains are frequently drawn, poles are the answer for heavy drapes, framing a window, or lightweight privacy curtains. More sophisticated poles may be fitted with draw-cords, gliders and decorative finials (those pretty end-pieces that stop the curtains from sliding off the pole). Prices will vary according to the style you choose.

Tracks range from simple, straight or curved styles to pricier, composite products which can support both curtains and a ruffled pelmet. These may have extension brackets to vary the distance between the curtains, walls and the pelmet.

If you are seeking a permanent arrangement, don't skimp on quality by using cheap, unreliable tracks. Remember to match hooks, gliders and end-stops to the style of curtain-heading tape

you have chosen. Pelmets hide a multitude of sins and save money because you can fit plainer tracks or rods than those required by exposed curtain heads.

Beautiful curtains must sit squarely on accurately positioned fittings. Arm yourself with a retractable fibreglass or metal tape measure and carefully measure window dimensions, frame size and the distance to the ceiling, floor and corners of adjacent walls. These measurements are essential when planning special effects, such as creating an impression of height on a shallow window. You can do this by hanging long curtains from poles or tracks raised well above the natural top of the window or even suspended from the ceiling.

Always anchor rods or tracks firmly with strong brackets, screwed to wooden battens or wall plugs. You will need to find out what's underneath your wall or ceiling plaster. If you arrange a free measure and quote from several reputable curtain makers (who will have to determine the construction materials to calculate costs), you'll be able to compare their prices and ask all your questions at no cost!

If you can avoid it, don't hang new curtains on old tracks or

poles. Choose fittings appropriate to the shape and style of your curtains. Heavy curtains may require special reinforcement, especially if they will be frequently opened and closed. Purchased kits should contain everything you'll need to complete the job: poles or tracks, strong brackets, sufficient hooks and gliders, and screws long enough to anchor brackets. Very long poles and tracks may need extra supporting brackets spaced at intervals between the usual end and centre brackets.

Choose fittings that frame your windows beautifully and do their job. Heavy curtains should completely retract to maximise light. For recessed windows, select flexible or curved metal tracks to fit the shape of the modern bay windows, hung with one continuous curtain or three separate curtains. Traditional bay windows, in three sections separated by wide corner frames, can use a single track or three separate curtain poles.

Instead of end-stops or finials, fit the last hook to a wall-mounted ring-fitting to hide track ends and avoid ugly gaps between curtains and walls. Never hang curtains straight across the face of a recessed window: they darken the room and detract from the charm of a traditional bay or dormer window.

Borders and Trims

Introduce the personal touch to soft furnishings with wonderful braids and trims. Today's furnishings are increasingly ornate and generous in proportion. There is a pronounced trend towards softness and fullness in design, whether it's in the lines of well-padded sofas and soft feather-filled cushions or generous metres of fabric, draped across curtains to form swagged pelmets or gathered into festoon blinds.

Interior designers have always valued the extra 'something' given to a piece of furniture or accessory by the addition of well chosen trims. Most stockists of furnishing fabrics have a good range of trims to choose from, and many are surprisingly inexpensive. While cost is a most important consideration, if only because it is possible to over-trim an inexpensive fabric, there are several other considerations to bear in mind when selecting your borders and trims.

Matching of styles is important. Common sense is the key here, and while creativity frequently challenges rules of colour and suitability, your 'eye' will tell you if a trim matches a fabric. Fabrics that are generally dull rather than lustrous tend to look casual – while shimmery fabrics will always have a more formal look. You need to look at trims in the same way. Simple rickrack braid will look smart but informal, and so too will bias binding, twill braids, checked ribbons and cotton laces.

Lustrous formal looks are enhanced by adding twisted silk cords and tassels, brocaded braids, metallic bindings and moire taffeta and silk ribbons. Some decorators manage to achieve wonderful 'surprises' by the unusual marriage of trims and fabric. It takes considerable skill to pull this off successfully, so take care.

Too much of a contrasting trim will become the focal point. If this is not your intention, be conscious of the impact of the trim you are adding. This is not a problem if the trim is in the same colour as your fabric. In this case it will not compete with the fabric, rather it will add interesting textured effects.

Will the braid be as long-wearing as the fabric? This may not be a major consideration, but if your fabric is expensive you will have to consider the life expectancy of your trims. Be mindful of where you use the trim – hand and headrests are more prone to wearing than the back of a sofa. It is sometimes a good idea to purchase more braid than you need right at the beginning to allow for replacement of worn areas.

Is the braid washable? Will the colour run in water? If you are planning to wash the trimmed item, you should wash the trim and the fabric first. This also applies if you are trimming an existing item – it will save you heartache later if you check shrinkage and colour fastness now. Sometimes a handful of household cooking salt thrown into cold rinsing water will help to 'set' dyes in trims, but it is always wise to be sure.

Creating
a look

*R*e-create your favourite decorating style at home with clever combinations of colour, texture and accessories. You may have to start with your existing rooms and furniture and ring the changes with our tips. Of course, if you are able to buy new furniture and fittings, it will certainly make your job a lot easier.

IKEA

Country Form

Three Great Looks

Classic

You can fake the elegant lines and smooth textures of the classic look by using single colour themes and rich-looking synthetic fabrics. Oval coffee and side tables, polished timber cabinets and wall mirrors, reflecting floor-length curtains and swags,

The Australian Wool Corporation

Dupont

Above: This elegant, classic living room shows the clever use of a subdued colour scheme and occasional furniture, lamps and ornaments to create the look
Left: The classic dining room features traditionally styled furniture, drapes and subtle lighting

develop this formal style. Repeat curtain colour in synthetic taffeta lamp shades, piped cushions trimmed with small tassels, or in graceful accessories like Grandma's favourite vase, a soft floral painting or a beautiful piece of glass. Plan formal arrangements of old-fashioned roses, camellias, gladioli and iris or stand spathiphyllum, strelitzia, flowering cyclamen, begonia or anthuriums in highly polished brass or timber planters. Conceal clutter in cupboards and light the rooms with traditional table or standard lamps, recessed spot lights, pendants or wall sconces – but keep it simple.

Contemporary

Simple lines and the smooth, cool textures of brushed or polished metals, glass, acrylic, polished timber and marble veneers reflect a no-fuss, contemporary approach. Upholstery options include leather or vinyl, linen or wool, lustrous satins or synthetics. The look is tailored and functional, without much fabric and absolutely no frills! Simple drapes and cushions in strong contrasting or neutral colours work with Roman and bonded blinds, slimline venetians or vertical drapes. Choose one or two accessories to develop the

theme, such as an abstract poster or print or a slim ceramic vase. Strike a green note with a single kentia palm, yucca or pony tail plant in a streamlined container. Compose simple floral arrangements of stark foliage and one beautiful lily or strelitzia in simple glass, ceramic or terracotta containers. Abundant natural light is a feature of the contemporary look, augmented with track lighting and floor or table lamps on slim adjustable stands. Use geometric pendants or spotlights to highlight important features in a room. Stereo and video equipment, books and collectables stand on open shelving or in glass cabinets, but take care to conceal the clutter in cupboards.

Country

Imitate the country folk who traditionally gather to make their own decorations with bright colours and lots of texture. Soften chunky pine or scrubbed timber furniture with tiny floral print fabrics or earthy homespuns, calico and wool. Treat used furniture bargains with weathered paint techniques or team rustic cane with frilly cushions. Select fabrics to complement existing colour schemes and add a touch of lace, a valance or handmade rag rug to achieve that country look. Accessorise with bright china plates hanging on walls; wreaths of dried grasses and seedpods framing small mirrors; toss a patchwork quilt on a sofa, bed or on a wall; hat and coat racks, watercolours and collections of almost anything from pebbles to milk jugs. Bunches of daisies, forget-me-nots or pansies and hanging baskets of ivy or maidenhair complement clustered pots of herbs, ferns and flowering geraniums or cineraria. Storage is open and cheerful. Have your shining pots stand on open dressers but camouflage modern appliances. Allow lots of natural light and at night, turn on soft table lamps, cane-shaded pendants or electric 'oil' lamps.

Right: This living room features the fabric, accessories and comfortable feel of the country style
Below: Natural timbers and stoneware accessories decorate this country kitchen
Below left: Simple lines and an absence of clutter are the marks of a contemporary room

Laura Ashley (Australia) Pty Limited

Country Form

IKEA

Personal Touches

Put the mark of your own personality into your decorating scheme. Your home, whether it's a big house or a rented room, should say something about you and your life.

The possibilities for adding that special, personal touch are as endless as your imagination. If you have a hobby, why not display your finished work, and even those pieces you are still working on, on a table or dresser top. Sometimes a pleasing display of an assortment of objects that you enjoy looking at, makes a wonderful decorating and personal statement.

Don't be too worried about the tidiness of your display or even how odd it may look. Be adventurous and you will be surprised at how much your visitors will enjoy looking at it and what a great ice-breaker it can be when entertaining.

Above: If you have odd pieces of unusual china that you've acquired over the years, don't hide it away in a cupboard but display it for everyone to admire

Right: An eclectic mixture of old Eastern brass, weights and measures and a delightful carved wooden shoe combined with the texture of an old water filter are sure conversation starters when displayed on this wooden mantle

Far right: A sunny corner blossoms with this arrangement of much loved bits and pieces and a lovely old bowl full of rosy onions

Above: Soften the hard look of a modern stairway with a display of old bottles, jars and even wheels
Above right: Dress up an open shelf with a handsome collection of rolling pins
Right: A few pieces of beautiful Chinese blue and white porcelain add the perfect finishing touch to any room

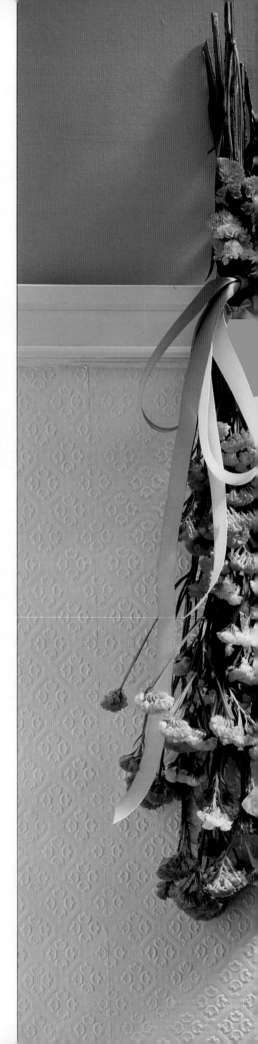

ways with Walls

*W*alls need not be finished with
plain paint any more. These days
you have an almost endless variety of
wallcoverings or wall finishes to choose
from and they need not break the
bank! You will find wallpapers for every
room in your home from scrubbable
vinyls for the kitchen to elegant flocked
papers for your dining room and pretty
florals for the bedroom. There are some
surprisingly easy methods of using
paint to create special effects, and the
best news is that they will add only a
little more to the initial cost of your
paint. All you need is a lot of
enthusiasm, a little energy and our
easy-to-follow Down to Detail
instructions for stencilling, ragging
and sponging.

Down to DETAIL

Wall Finishes

Sponging

This is one of the quickest and easiest ways of achieving a broken colour effect on walls and woodwork. Your base coat should be emulsion or acrylic paint in a light colour. Your second and subsequent colours are either brighter or darker and are applied by dabbing all over the base coat with a large natural sponge. You can use several tones of the one colour for a subtle finished effect. If you intend to sponge several rooms with different colours, it is a good idea to keep one sponge for each colour. Do not use paint directly from the paint tin. Pour a small amount into a shallow tray to prevent the sponge becoming overloaded with paint.

Above: Applying the second coat with a fresh sponge
Left: Applying the base coat in a random pattern, using a sponge

Relief papers

This traditional wallpaper has a long decorative history. The paper is pressed over rollers leaving an all over raised pattern which stays permanently in place. The thickness of the paper makes it ideal for disguising any imperfections in walls, and is the ideal treatment for the area between traditional chair rails (dado) and skirting boards.

Once the paper is dry, paint it to match or contrast with the rest of the room. Relief papers are most inexpensive and are not pre-pasted.

Ragging

This is a very quick and effective way to achieve an interesting effect on a plain wall, using a scrunched-up, lint-free rag or even a plastic bag. You may find some team effort worthwhile here, as the effect depends on the top coat of paint being 'lifted

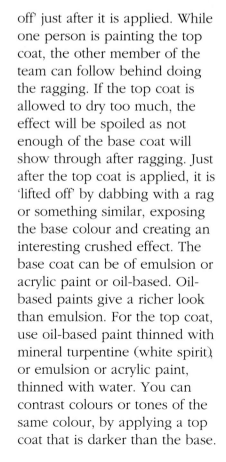

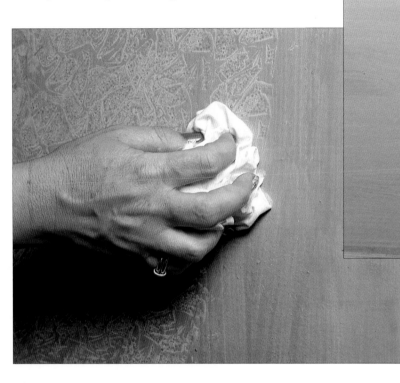

off' just after it is applied. While one person is painting the top coat, the other member of the team can follow behind doing the ragging. If the top coat is allowed to dry too much, the effect will be spoiled as not enough of the base coat will show through after ragging. Just after the top coat is applied, it is 'lifted off' by dabbing with a rag or something similar, exposing the base colour and creating an interesting crushed effect. The base coat can be of emulsion or acrylic paint or oil-based. Oil-based paints give a richer look than emulsion. For the top coat, use oil-based paint thinned with mineral turpentine (white spirit) or emulsion or acrylic paint, thinned with water. You can contrast colours or tones of the same colour, by applying a top coat that is darker than the base.

Down to DETAIL

Stencilling

Stencilling is one of the oldest decorative effects and can be as simple or ornate as you wish. Traditionally, stencils were cut from oiled cardboard or even brass sheets and were regarded as a craftsman's tools. Today you can still use brass and cardboard stencils but inexpensive plastic stencils are now readily available in an enormous variety of contemporary and traditional designs. You can also design and cut your own stencil using a plastic sheet and tracing your chosen design with a chinagraph pencil or a fine, indelible, felt-tipped pen.

Before You Begin

❏ It is important to use the correct brush for stencilling – an ordinary paint brush will not do. Stencil brushes are flat-topped and are used by dabbing the brush down onto the area to be coloured, rather than stroking. This prevents paint being pushed under the stencil edges and smearing the design. You can use small natural sponges.

❏ As for your paints, it is best to use acrylic or special fast-drying stencil paint. If mixing colours to achieve a desired tint, mix enough for the entire room, as it is difficult to duplicate a particular colour

mix. Take care too that your paints are very creamy in consistency, so they will not clog the brush or sponge, but not so thin that they will run under the stencil edges. If you are stencilling in more than one colour and are concerned that the colours should not run into one another, paints can be dried quickly with a hairdryer on low force and medium heat.

❏ If stencilling with more than one colour, it is a good idea to cover with masking tape those parts of the stencil design to be painted in the second colour. Wait for the first colour to dry before stencilling with the second one and so on. This will stop one colour from bleeding into the other.

Top: Applying the first colour of the stencilled border to the wall
Above: Applying the second colour to complete the stencilled design

Stencilling a border

MATERIALS

- ☐ suitable paint
- ☐ stencil brushes
- ☐ manila cards
- ☐ linseed oil
- ☐ mineral turpentine (white spirit)
- ☐ sharp craft knife
- ☐ cutting board
- ☐ pencils
- ☐ plumb line
- ☐ spirit level
- ☐ chalk
- ☐ masking tape

METHOD

Make the stencil in the same way as for the Stencilled Floorcloth on page 42.

1 Paint the wall in the normal way. Then, using a plumb line and spirit level, mark the position of your border, marking both horizontal and vertical base lines.

2 Place the stencil on the wall, aligning its edges with the drawn lines and marking each corner of the stencil with easily-removed blackboard chalk. Continue placing the stencil along the guidelines, marking the corners along the entire length of the border.

3 Attach the stencil to the wall with masking tape. If you are using more than one colour, cover over any areas to be painted in another colour with masking tape to avoid paint overlapping.

4 Be sure to remove any excess paint from your brush or sponge before applying it to the wall. You will find surprisingly little paint is needed. Work in circular movements from the centre of each cutout area to the edges. Part of the charm of a stencilled decoration is the variations that occur in paint application, so don't feel compelled to paint until a solid block of colour appears, or to match one motif exactly to the next.

5 When the paint is dry, unmask the stencil and clean it if necessary. Then move the stencil to the next set of chalk marks and paint as before. Continue in this way until the border is completed.

Left: Use this stencil design at any size you like. Simply enlarge it on a photocopying machine to your preferred size

Decorating with Wallpaper

There are not many do-it-yourself activities that will give you more satisfaction than wallpapering. And it really is easy!

Vinyl-based wallpapers (which come prepasted and ready to put straight on the wall) make paper-hanging so easy that even first-timers can produce quite professional results.

Wallpapering is particularly satisfying because the rewards are so immediate and dramatic. In just a day or two you can transform a tired bedroom, a bland living room or a problem hallway. What's more, the wallpaper comes off the wall as easily as it went on, so in a few years if you feel like a change – hey presto and it's a whole new look.

Use wallpapers and borders to inject life, colour, warmth and style into the gloomiest of rooms. Create a feeling of coolness in a room that becomes overheated easily and add warmth and cosiness to rooms that miss out on the sunlight.

Let your lifestyle and individual sense of design help you choose your wallpapers – and what a choice! Whether you are looking for a sophisticated city-style look for a new flat or a country cottage look for a house, there's a huge range of superb designs to cater for your taste. You can mix patterns and plains or even florals with stripes, paper below the chair rail or above it! It's up to you. One thing is certain – you'll have lots of fun!

How to choose your wallpaper

Most shops carry large 'libraries' of pattern books with entire ranges in a variety of colourways. However, you don't want to spend hours and days wading through sample books. This usually leads to confusion and much frustration!

Instead, take details of the rooms to be decorated, including their size; colour and style of the drapes, carpets and other furnishings; the direction windows face; colours of adjoining rooms. A good retailer will be able to show you an imaginative range of options. Don't be afraid to select something that reflects your personality and individuality. You could try one of the superb flocks: brilliant if you're lucky enough to have a chandelier. You might prefer a grasscloth – real or imitation – with its horizontal weave and texture which creates the illusion of the room being larger than it really is.

Still not sure? As well as pattern books, many retailers carry stocks of sample rolls and may allow you to take these home to see how the paper looks in the room it is destined for.

WHICH WALLPAPER TO CHOOSE?

❏ **Vinyl** is today's most popular wallpaper. Made from polyvinyl chloride (PVC) it is resistant to water and can be scrubbed with a soft bristle brush to remove most marks. It is usually prepasted.

❏ **Vinyl coated** papers have had liquid PVC applied to them, giving a more durable, washable surface.

❏ **Embossed vinyl** has been moulded to give a raised pattern and has a tough paper backing.

❏ **Blown vinyl** has a relief design effect, created by expanding the vinyl during manufacture.

❏ **Duplex** wallcovering consists of two sheets of paper which have been bonded for strength. It can be sponged but not scrubbed.

❏ **Natural papers**, such as grasscloth and silks, cork, wood veneers, burlap, are all made from natural materials applied to paper backings. Hanging them usually requires some degree of expertise.

❏ **Flock wallcoverings** are regarded as an elegant background for traditional decorating schemes. Finely chopped wool, rayon or nylon is applied to the design and coated with adhesive, for a luxurious velvet effect.

❏ **Relief papers** are usually white and not to be confused with the embossed vinyls or flocks. Relief papers include anaglypta, a great favourite in Victorian times. Anaglypta is made by bonding two sheets of paper then passing it through deeply-embossed rollers.

❏ **Mylar foil** is made from a resin. It looks like real foil but won't show creases after hanging.

❏ **Foil** is a thin, flexible metal sheet (often aluminium), laminated onto a backing of paper or fabric. Excellent for accent areas such as one wall of a bathroom or in a small hallway.

❏ **Murals** range from maps of the world to scenes of autumnal forests and tropical islands which can cover an entire wall, creating a feeling of spaciousness in small rooms.

Getting Started

Preparing the surface is important and well worth the effort. You should aim for clean, non-porous surfaces because porous surfaces 'steal' moisture from the paste, affecting its adhesive qualities. Different wall surfaces will require different kinds of preparation. Check with your local wallpaper shop for any specific instructions for your walls.

If possible, remove blinds and curtains, wall lights and, of course, prints and pictures! Give yourself the maximum room in which to work by moving furniture to another room or placing it in the centre. Use drop sheets to protect your floor coverings: old bed sheets are ideal.

If you intend papering the ceiling as well as the walls, do this first. If not, paint the ceiling and all woodwork before you begin papering.

Which room first?

Most people wallpapering for the first time choose a small room, such as the bathroom, in which to start…just in case! This is a mistake – you'll have a cistern, shower recess, bath, wash basin, cabinet and all sorts of other odd-shaped fittings to contend with and work around.

It's much easier to begin in a bedroom or lounge where the walls are uninterrupted, allowing you to quickly polish your skills. By the time you reach the bathroom, you'll be an expert!

Borders

Friezes or borders are very popular and have led to a revival of interest in all wallcoverings. To begin with, borders are inexpensive and simple to apply and remove. Success with a border will inspire a feeling of confidence and soon you'll want to paper an entire room.

The tools you'll need are the same as for wallpapering and the same rules apply for wall preparation as for wallpaper.

Measuring is easy too. It's all done in linear metres, so you simply measure the distance around a room. If it is going around a door, then measure the sides and top too. Most borders are sold in 5 or 10 m lengths so

Lifestyle

you get plenty for your money! They are often prepasted so you can use the water trough as you would with full-sized wallpaper.

Perhaps the most dramatic use of borders is at chair rail height. You can then paper below and paint above or vice-versa, or use two different but complementary wallpapers and have the border intersecting them.

You can apply a border over the top of wallpaper to provide focal points, or use a border to give added importance to a prized mirror, painting or print. You can even apply them to ceilings for a very distinctive designer look!

How much wallpaper do you need?

Walls		Distance around the room (doors and windows included)																
METRES		8.53	9.75	10.97	12.19	13.41	14.63	15.85	17.07	18.29	19.51	20.73	21.95	23.16	24.38	25.60	26.82	28.04	29.26
	FEET	28'	32'	36'	40'	44'	48'	52'	56'	60'	64'	68'	72'	76'	80'	84'	88'	92'	96'
2.13 to 2.29	6' 10" to 7' 6"	5	5	6	6	7	7	8	8	9	9	10	10	10	11	11	13	13	14
2.30 to 2.44	7' 7" to 8' 0"	5	5	6	6	7	7	8	9	9	10	10	11	11	12	13	14	14	15
2.45 to 2.59	8' 1" to 8' 6"	5	6	6	7	7	8	8	9	9	10	10	12	12	13	14	15	15	15
2.60 to 2.74	8' 7" to 9' 0"	5	6	6	7	7	8	9	9	10	10	11	13	13	14	14	15	15	16
2.75 to 2.90	9' 1" to 9' 6"	5	6	7	7	8	8	9	10	10	11	11	13	14	14	15	15	16	17
2.91 to 3.05	9' 7" to 10' 0"	6	6	7	8	8	9	10	10	11	11	12	14	14	15	16	16	17	17
3.06 to 3.20	10' 1" to 11' 6"	6	6	7	8	9	9	10	11	11	12	13	14	15	16	16	17	18	18
		Number of rolls required																	

A Roomful of Treasures

Long ago you were given a blue plate, then you bought another one at a local bazaar and then a friend gave you one for Christmas and, before you knew it, you had a collection! Your collection of plates, dolls, jelly moulds, tin cans, or whatever, offers great decorating possibilities if you display it well.

Perhaps you're a traveller and have brought back souvenirs that share a common theme – scarves, plates, luggage labels – you can frame or hang them on a dull wall. Ethnic collections can bring fascinating textures and colour to a room. Hand-loomed fabrics and carpets, primitive sculpture and hand-woven baskets will all complement each other.

Try to create a theme in certain rooms. An old favourite is a marine theme in bathrooms – shells collected from holidays long ago, framed shell prints and perhaps a mirror surrounded by shells. Libraries and studios lend themselves to collections of photographs, sporting trophies or memorabilia, and old prints. Kitchens are ideal for displaying utensils – old jelly moulds, ornate cake plates, bottle openers, scales with weights and measures, beverage bottles and old stoneware jars, all bring a rustic, cared-for and friendly look to a kitchen. If you are lucky enough to own one, an old timber dresser makes an ideal home for a kitchen collection. Collections of quite large objects, such as copper pans or baskets, can look wonderful suspended from the ceiling on hooks.

Above: A lovely collection of old millefleurs plates brings warmth to a plain white wall. See how the variety in shape and size adds interest to the display
Below: Kitchen ceilings are not usually very interesting to look at, except if they are like this one. A collection of stoneware milk jugs is suspended from timber beams

34

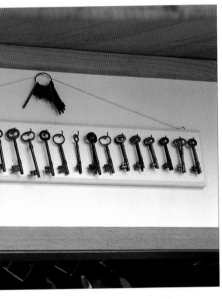

Top: A collection of antique ginger beer bottles line open shelves in a country-style kitchen. The warmth and colours of the stoneware add a pleasing feature to the room
Above: For a great sense of fun why not a collection of old keys of various shapes and sizes? Collected from junk shops, attics and church bazaars, they are mounted on a simple board using cup hooks

Collections in entrance halls make a great decorating statement. This is often the first impression visitors get about the owners of the house and your first chance to show off! Our photograph of old-fashioned vases, shaped like hats, shows a colourful and whimsical touch, especially when it's complemented by a large bunch of spring blooms in a quaint old jug. Take care though, if you have small children and a large dog, a table in the narrow entrance hall may not be the ideal place to display a precious collection of china.

Above: This is a truly charming and unusual collection of vases in the shape of fancy hats, carefully mounted on a plain wall

Some collections just evolve or you can set out quite deliberately to assemble objects in a decorative group. Sometimes items from different eras can be combined successfully, but keep a colour or theme link between them. Old theatre programmes, nautical bits and pieces, books, paintings of a particular subject, coloured china, fashion accessories or toys are all varied and delightful when gathered and displayed in interesting collections.

Framing Up

Bare walls just cry out for the decorator's touch and pictures are the obvious solution. The right frame for your picture and the arrangement of a group of plates can make all the difference. These are some very clever decorator's tricks for framing your prints or paintings.

Above: This charming collection of old black and white prints is not what it seems. If you look closely, you will see that the pictures, the frames and the ornate hanging bows and drapes are in fact applied directly to the wall
Left: Give new life to an old picture frame rescued from the junk shop with the use of a little gold paint and some fancy ribbon
Above centre: Another frame salvaged from the junk heap hides behind this border of glued-on shells
Above left: Frame a group of china plates by stencilling a pattern of bows and tassels on the wall behind
Far Left: Follow through the folk-art theme of these hand-stitched samplers with rustic styled frames like these. It is important that your frame reflects the style and feeling of the art.

what's Afoot?

*W*hatever you choose for floor coverings, it will be a substantial investment, so don't rush into it. Quality ranges from the very basic to the luxurious, and there are attractive options at both ends of the scale and in between.

All about Floors

Carpets

Laying fitted carpets (wall-to-wall or broadloom) should be left to professional carpet layers but large carpet squares, rugs and carpet tiles are portable, easy to lay and can be repositioned to spread the wear. Fibres can be man-made or natural: acrylic and polyester, nylon, wool or wool blends. Nylon is durable and versatile, wool is a natural insulator and less prone to static electricity; stains, dust and burns are less noticeable. Popular wool-nylon blends display the advantages of both fibres. Pile also affects wear and appearance. Loop-pile is tougher than the plush surface of beautiful cut-pile carpets which mark easily. Combination cut-and-loop or sturdy cut-and-twist offer interesting patterns and textures. Modern, easy-care rubber-backed carpets are available in attractive colours and patterns featuring a variable density of pile for different purposes. They're durable and comfortable to stand on.

Right: Slate floors in one of the many beautiful colours available are an ideal choice for a kitchen floor
Below: Pure wool fitted carpet enhances the open plan of this lovely living/dining room

Ceramic tiles

This is the perfect choice for anyone needing a low maintenance, easy-to-clean flooring but their highly glazed surface may be slippery when wet, something to remember when choosing bathroom or kitchen tiles. Ceramic tiles retain heat in winter yet stay deliciously cool in summer. They come in different sizes, from the very small to the very large. Generally, large tiles should be installed by professionals, as should those on awkward floors where you need to cut tiles to fit around built-in units and plumbing. The amount you save by laying them yourself can easily be swallowed up in the cost of replacing badly cut or damaged tiles. Remember too, that ceramic tiles give you no second chance for that dropped plate or vase. If you are a bit of a 'butter fingers' or have small children, this may not be a wise choice for you.

Amber Tiles

Dupont

Slate

The colours and textures of slate enhance any setting. It stays cool in summer and warm in winter. You'll need a diamond-tipped saw to cut slate but its irregular texture will camouflage accidents. You must allow time for slate bedded in sand and cement to dry thoroughly, then sweep away mineral salts before sealing. Clean with a mop and warm water.

Lifestyle

Above: For a truly dramatic effect, you can lay ceramic tiles in patterns like this one
Above right: The natural warmth of polished timber floors enhances any room setting

Coir, seagrass and sisal matting

Tough, grassy fibres wear well, have great texture and lovely natural colours. They're do-it-yourself favourites but moisture can cause mildew, rotting and unpleasant odours. Matting should last around ten years with regular cleaning to prevent fibre damage from built-up grit and sand in the matting.

Cork tiles

A relatively short-term option for kitchens and playrooms, cork cushions tired feet and once sealed is easily cleaned with a moist, soft mop. Cork is less durable than vinyl and is generally only good for one 'recut' (resand) and reseal before needing replacement.

Rubber tiles

Brightly-coloured, high-tech tiles that are easy to lay and cut into patterns. Noise-absorbing, they are ideal for playrooms, kitchens and other high traffic areas. Rubber is non-slip and impervious to moisture. It's kind to tired legs and easy to clean.

Terracotta tiles

Richly-coloured, clay-based terracotta is an attractive choice and a sound investment, requiring little maintenance after sealing: just clean with a soft mop and a few drops of white vinegar in water. See the caution about early sealing of slate floors – the same applies to tiles. Do take care when working with tools or moving furniture as a dropped hammer or other heavy object can damage any highly glazed floor tile.

Wood

Timber floors are beautiful and once sealed, they are easy to clean, very durable and can be left unadorned or strewn with rugs. Timber strip floors are constructed from either hardwood (wears forever and comes in striking natural colours with little grain) or softwood (less durable but features lovely grain and knots, best for light traffic areas). Noise-absorbing parquet flooring panels are easy to lay and ideal for kitchens or family rooms. They wear quickly in high traffic areas and may need recutting and resealing about once every three years. Sweep timber floors with a soft broom and never use detergents or solvents on them. A few drops of fabric conditioner in a bucket of warm water, applied with a soft, moist (not wet) mop, can give a lovely finish.

Vinyl

Choose either tiles or sheets (in different widths) in a multitude of colours and patterns, including superb slate and marble look-alikes. Vinyl tiles are thinner and more brittle than sheets but easier to fit around difficult angles, and errors are less expensive because you only damage one or two tiles rather than a whole sheet. Their coarse finish scratches easily, recovers slowly from dents and needs more maintenance: not a good choice for busy rooms. Vinyl sheets are denser and more resilient: they recover faster from furniture and heel impressions. Some sheets feature cushion backing while some have a built-in sealant. Sheeting is more pliable than tiles and easier on the legs in kitchens and playrooms.

Stencilled Floorcloth

*Painted or stencilled floorcloths were popular in the 18th and
19th centuries as a cheap and colourful way to decorate the floors.
Traditionally made of canvas and painted with housepaint, the
cloths had a brittle surface which had a tendency to crack and
discolour over a period of time. The availability of modern,
fast-drying acrylic paints, and even specialised fabric inks, makes
floorcloth decoration easier and gives greater durability.*

Before You Begin

❏ When choosing your paints, it is advisable to use opaque inks, especially when printing onto a dark background.

❏ We recommend you make two chequerboard stencils because of the amount of stencilling to be done. The inks tend to build up on the stencils during use, thus reducing the size of the design.

❏ For small areas, use either a small stencil brush or even a cotton bud.

❏ You can cut separate stencils for each part of the design or mask off areas to be painted in a different colour with masking tape if using a single stencil.

❏ Primed artists' canvas can be used and does not need undercoat.

❏ Planning on graph paper helps with dimensions and corner placement.

❏ For background or undercoat for this floorcloth, we used transparent base for opaque screen printing inks (available through screen printing suppliers) but matt acrylic varnish or PVA adhesive glue (1 part glue:5 parts water) can also be used.

MATERIALS

The materials and measurements given here will make a floorcloth with finished measurements of 160 cm x 1 m.

For the floorcloth:
☐ 1.5 m of 180 cm wide heavy cotton canvas
☐ screen printing inks or acrylic paints in your choice of colours

- matt varnish (polyurethane) to seal the finished surface
- contact adhesive
- coloured pencils in the same colours as your paints
- 1.5 cm wide masking tape

For the stencil:

- one 11.5 cm square manila card for the corner flower design; one 22 cm square manila card for the centre flower design; two 20 cm x 40 cm manila cards for the chequerboard design
- linseed oil
- mineral turpentine (white spirit)
- fine lead pencil
- eraser for removing pencil markings
- stencil brushes (small and medium sized) or sponges
- craft knife or sharp blade
- board or piece of glass on which to cut stencils

METHOD

See Pull Out Pattern Sheet at the back of the book for the small floral and the chequerboard stencils. See page 75 for the large floral stencil.

For the stencils:

1 Draw two diagonal lines from corner to corner on each of the four blank pieces of manila card. The intersection of these lines indicates the centre of each manila card.

2 Coat both sides of each manila card generously with a 50:50 mixture of linseed oil and mineral turpentine (white spirit) and allow to dry. Remove any excess oiliness by wiping with a soft cloth.

3 To trace the stencil designs onto your oiled manila cards, position the corner flower design in the centre of the 11.5 cm square card and the centre flower design in the centre of the 22 cm square and trace.

4 Draw a grid of 2.5 cm squares on the other two pieces of card, leaving a 5 cm border all around the edge of each card. Try to keep the chequerboard measurements as accurate as possible. Cut out alternate squares of the chequerboard pattern. At the 5 cm border line, cut a notch in each edge of the stencil cards, as shown on the Pattern Sheet. These notches will help you align the chequerboard pattern.

For the floorcloth:

1 Cut the sheet of canvas to measure 180 cm x 120 cm. This includes hem allowances of 10 cm.

2 Lay the canvas out on a large flat surface, and weight or tack down the edges. Measure in 10 cm from each side and draw a fine pencil line. This is your hem marking.

3 Place masking tape *outside* this rectangle with your tape edge along the pencil line. Using your undercoat or background colour, paint the canvas inside this taped rectangle and allow it to dry.

4 Place a second piece of tape butting up against the inside edge of the first row of tape. Place a third row of tape, butting its edge up to the inside edge of the second. Remove the middle row of tape and put it aside for later use. This process will give you the correct size and location for painting the perimeter stripe. Cut away the tape overlap at the corners to give an uninterrupted border line.

5 With green paint/ink, paint the stripe between the rows of masking tape. Allow to dry. Before removing the masking tape, trace around the inside edges with a fine pencil line. This will be where you will begin your chequerboard pattern.

6 Position your 11.5 cm square piece of manila card in a corner with two sides of the card butted up against the inside edge of the masking tape. Trace around the outside of the card with a fine pencil line and repeat this procedure in each corner. This area will be used for stencilling the corner flower design.

7 Position your chequerboard design with the notches in the short side edges aligned along the fine pencil line. Using a coloured pencil to match colour 1, trace around the inside of your stencil in the areas where you wish to use that colour. Position the stencil for colour 2 and using an appropriately-coloured pencil, repeat the procedure.

8 Place the first chequerboard stencil back on the canvas, with the coloured lines as your guide and using a stencil brush or sponge, apply the appropriate colour with a dabbing motion. Allow the paint to dry and repeat the process using the second chequerboard stencil and the second colour.

9 When the chequerboard pattern is dry, position the corner flower stencils, matching the edges of the card to the edges of the chequerboard pattern. Paint in the first colour. Place the same stencil in the diagonally opposite corner and paint in the same colour. Paint the second colour in the other corners.

10 Position three rows of masking tape as before, this time *inside* the edge of the chequerboard design. Once again, remove the centre row of tape, and paint the green stripe as before.

Centre design

To make a placement line for the central flower stencil, draw a line lengthways, down the centre of the floorcloth. Place the larger flower design stencil diagonally on this line, with the stem towards the centre and as close as possible to the inner border pattern. Place a small mark on the cloth where one corner of the card is nearest the centre. This is important, as it shows you where to position the card for the next flower, which is one step closer to the centre. Apply the paint with a light dabbing motion. Repeat this procedure, starting from the opposite end. You should then have four flower motifs along the centre line, with their stems towards the centre.

If you prefer to cluster the flowers in the centre, draw two centre guidelines, one lengthways and the other across the width. Simply place the stencil in each quarter with the stem towards the centre.

To complete:

1 When all the stencilling is completed and the ink is dry, carefully iron the floorcloth with a hot, *dry* iron. You must either iron the floorcloth on the wrong side or use a pressing cloth.

2 Fold under the hem allowances and glue them in place, mitring corners. Place something heavy on the glued edges to ensure a good bond while it is drying.

3 Coat the right side of the floorcloth with two or three coats of clear lacquer (acrylic or polyurethane) to protect and seal. If you are planning to store your floorcloth, it is best rolled not folded.

Floor Finishes

If your floors are looking a bit sad and worn, don't decide immediately on covering them with fitted carpets. Often the solution to unattractive floors is a creative one, rather than a bank-breaking exercise! The methods for transforming basic floor boards are simple and inexpensive, and well within the capabilities of the home handyperson.

Whichever method you choose, you will first need to fill all the knot holes with a proprietary wood filler and seal the finished, treated floor boards with clear polyurethane paint.

Bleaching

Bleaching will result in a much lighter floor colour that can be sealed with polyurethane paint. The method is most suitable for floors that have not been stained, as stain soaks into the fibres of the timber and is difficult to eliminate completely although bleaching can lighten an existing stain. If the timber has been treated with stain and a polyurethane sealer in the past, it must be first sanded back to the stained timber.

Ensure good ventilation while you're working, as the fumes from bleach can be irritating.

METHOD

1 Paint the floor with liquid bleach and allow it to soak into the timber. Continue to coat the floor with bleach until the desired lightness is achieved. This may be a slow process. After bleaching, wash the floor down with a 50:50 solution of white vinegar and water to neutralise the bleach. If the timber swells during bleaching, it is easily overcome with light sanding.

2 Seal with clear polyurethane paint following the maker's instructions.

Staining

Staining does not have to be restricted to the traditional wood shades – you can be quite adventurous with your colour choices!

METHOD

1 Select the stain colour of your choice. If the floor is new, or has been freshly sanded, apply the colour as the manufacturer directs.

2 If you have an existing stained and sealed floor, you will need to sand the floor back to a raw state, then proceed to stain with a new colour as the stain maker directs.

Floor finishes from left to right: Bleached; limed and stencilled; stained and stencilled; limed; stained

3 Once you are satisfied with the colour achieved, seal the floor with clear polyurethane paint following maker's instructions.

Stencilling

This decorative method of painting floors has stood the test of time! Creative people have long painted their floors, not only to save money, but to be able to enjoy a continuation of the design theme in their room. So often the floor is regarded only as a platform for the room, when it could be a decorative feature in its own right. Stencilling can be done over a previously stained and sealed floor.

Borders work very well on floors, especially as a frame for feature rugs. They can emphasise areas of the room, by giving visual definition to various sections, such as around fireplaces.

METHOD

1 Sand back the surface of the floor where the paint is to be applied sufficiently to give a rough feel. This roughness will allow the stencil paint to adhere to the floor without the risk of it flaking off.

2 Following our directions for STENCILLING A BORDER on page 31, mark out where your decorated areas will be. When you are happy with the placement, draw in your guidelines and stencil in the designs.

3 When the stencilled areas are completely dry, seal with clear polyurethane paint following the maker's instructions.

Painted floors

This method of revamping a floor works very well in low-traffic areas, or in rooms that have a large central area covered by a rug. You can paint high-traffic areas, but you must be prepared for the paint to wear away quickly in these areas. You may choose to paint with acrylic paints, wiping off the paint shortly after application in the direction of the grain using a lint-free cloth.

METHOD

1 Paint can be applied over existing stain and sealer, but you will need to sand back any obvious rough areas before starting to paint.

2 Be sure that you don't fall into the trap of painting yourself into a corner! Start painting at the furthest corner from the door, and work back towards the door.

3 Making certain that the floor is dust-free, paint the floor with several coats of oil-based paint. Sanding back lightly between coats of paint will encourage the better adherence of subsequent coats of paint.

4 Finally, seal the floor with one or two coats of clear polyurethane paint, following the maker's instructions.

Seating
arrangements

W*ell, you've papered the walls, chosen your floor coverings and now it's time to look at your furnishings. New living room furniture can be very costly so investigate what alternatives are available. Big floor cushions are probably the most economical solution to the seating problem, though not necessarily the most comfortable. They are quite simple to make and you can discard them later as you replace them with more substantial pieces.*

If you already have a sofa which is looking a bit 'tired', consider having it recovered, or better still, doing the job yourself. Do-it-yourself upholstery requires a lot of patience and some specific skills. Check out your local community college or night classes for a suitable course, or the local library for a book with good step-by-step directions. If this still sounds a bit out of your league, then our convertible sofa bed is the perfect answer to your problem. No special skills are necessary, just some readily available raw materials and your sewing machine. (See page 48)

IKEA

Sofa Bed and Pillows

In the wink of an eye, this very clever sofa changes into a double bed for those unexpected guests. It would look just as good covered in a geometric print, denim or traditional mattress ticking.

Before You Begin

❏ The size of your sofa bed is pretty much up to you. We have used a double bed-size piece of foam, cut into four pieces. You may prefer to buy the four pieces already cut, if these are available.

❏ We have used foam that is approximately 15 cm thick. If your foam is a different thickness, adjust your fabric measurements accordingly.

MATERIALS

☐ piece of foam approximately 137 cm x 183 cm x 15 cm thick
☐ 7 m of 180 cm wide plain desuti, light-weight canvas, denim or heavy calico
☐ 5 m of 4 cm wide firm, cotton webbing tape or twill tape
☐ 2 pillows
☐ one double bed feather or polyester-filled continental quilt
☐ 12 mm wide coloured cotton tape, enough to stitch around the outside edges of the quilt and down each channel and around the pillowcases. One side of an average double quilt will use about 35 m

METHOD

1.5 cm seams allowed throughout.

1 Measure the foam and mark crossways cutting lines to divide it into four equal blocks – each approximately 137 cm x 46.5 cm x 15 cm. To cut foam, it is best to use an electric carving knife or jigsaw and to raise the foam up on house bricks.

2 Make paper patterns of the sides, ends, top and bottom surfaces. Add

1.5 cm seam allowances all around each piece. Cut 8 side panels, 8 end panels, 8 top/bottom panels. Cut 2 pillowcases, each 1.75 cm x 50 cm.

3 Mark each one of the four foam blocks A, B, C and D.

To cover blocks A and D:

1 Take two side pieces and two end pieces and join the short ends together to form a strip then join the ends to form an open rectangular box. (See Fig. 1)

2 On the right side of the fabric, sew a length of webbing tape to one long edge of one side piece, starting and ending 1.5 cm from both corner seams, with the tape lapping over the edge of the fabric by about 2 cm. (See Fig. 1)

3 Pin the top panel to the box, matching corners to seams and stitch all around. Pin the bottom panel to the other side of the box and sew on three sides – leaving the taped side open. (See Fig. 2)

To cover block B:

1 Join side and end panels as for A and D (see Fig. 1). Sew one length of webbing tape to one long side panel as for A and D.

2 Take a top edge of the opposite long panel and stitch it to the webbing protruding from block A, still leaving the seam open. Attach the top and bottom panels, still leaving the taped edge open. Turn the cover right side out.

To cover block C:

1 Join side and end panels into an open box as for B but do not sew on any tape. Stitch top and bottom panels to sides, leaving open one top edge and one

diagonally opposite bottom edge of the long side panels. Join to cushion D in the same way as A and B. Turn CD right side out. This gives you two hinged pairs AB and CD. (See Fig. 3)

2 Handstitch the AB pair of cushions to the CD pair, by inserting the tape from B into the still-open seam in C, so that they will fold in an M or W shape when viewed from the end. (See Fig. 4)

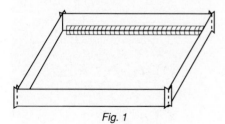

Fig. 1

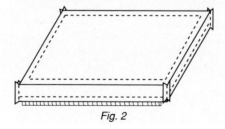

Fig. 2

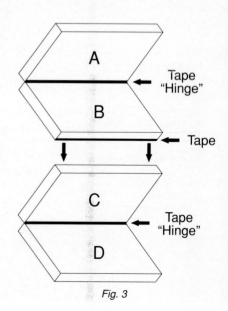

Fig. 3

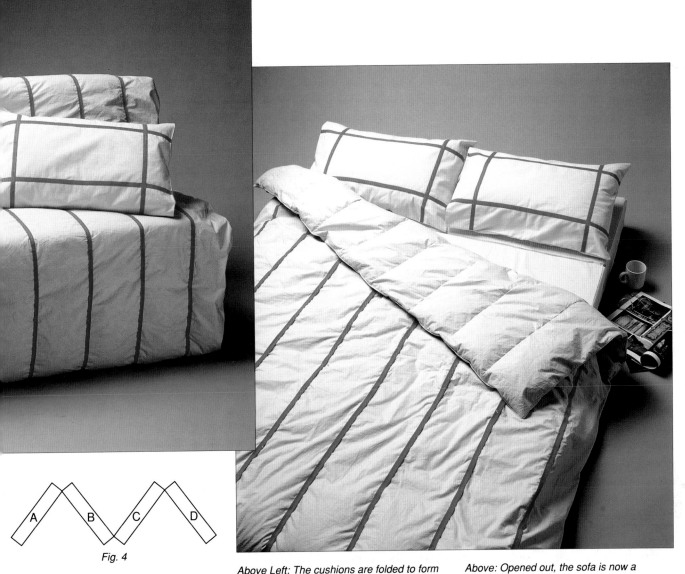

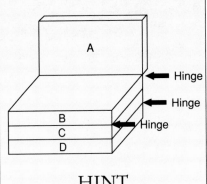

Fig. 4

Above Left: The cushions are folded to form the sofa and covered with the trimmed quilt

Above: Opened out, the sofa is now a comfortable bed

3 Ease the foam blocks inside the covers at the hinged openings. Fold under each opening seam allowance and slipstitch it to the tape, so that the cover fits snugly and the connecting seam is closed.

4 Placed about 10 cm from the wall, the top cushion flips up to form the back of the sofa and converts easily to a double bed.

For the pillowcases:

1 Turn under 6 mm on the short ends of the fabric. Turn under another 1 cm. Stitch down and press. Fold 5 cm under on one end. Stitch in place. Fold 15 cm under on the other end. Pin side seams. Match the two ends together and press. Remove pins.

2 Measure 12 cm from both folds and top and bottom edges. Mark these lines with dressmaker's chalk. Pin col-

oured tape around the rectangles as marked. Stitch tape into place, mitring its corners as you go. You will have a border of tape on both sides of the pillowcase.

3 Fold the trimmed pillowcase as shown on page 77 with right sides facing. Stitch sides. Take care to secure the stitching well at the open end. Turn to right side and press.

Throwover quilt

We have decorated an inexpensive, purchased quilt for use with the sofa bed. During the day it provides an attractive cover and at night can be slipped into a single bed quilt cover. Stitch coloured tape around all the edges and down the channels of the quilt. You can stitch this on one side only or on both, as you prefer.

HINT

An easy way to see how the sofa hinges, is to tape together four empty audio cassette cases, marked A, B, C and D, according to the diagrams. You will find it helpful to refer to this while you are making the sofa.

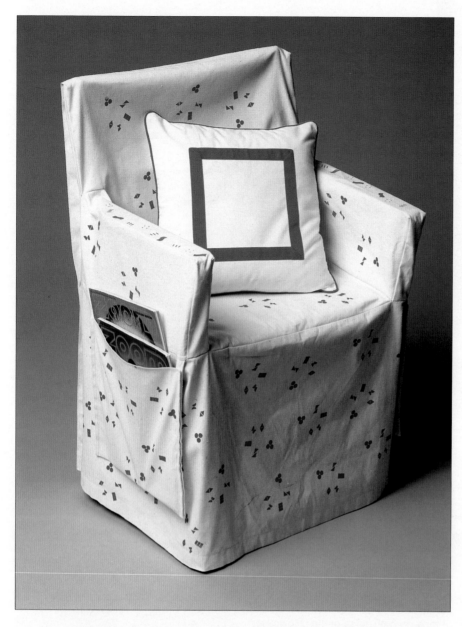

Trimmed cushions are the ideal companion for the covered Director's Chair. Make a cushion following the directions for the Heirloom Cushions, page 52, omitting the frill. Before assembling, stitch braid around cushion front, folding the braid into a mitre at each corner

Director's Chair Cover

The director's chair has found a place in many households at one time or another. Reasonably priced, comfortable and easy to store, it can undergo endless transformations. This is a great way to dress up a director's chair. Whether you choose a plain fabric such as ours or a bold print, these inexpensive chairs will take on a whole new look.

❏ The pattern pieces for this slipcover are on the Pull Out Pattern Sheet at the back of the book. Cut out all the pieces with the right dimensions and label them.

MATERIALS

☐ 2.2 m of 150 cm wide heavy-duty cotton fabric
☐ matching sewing thread
☐ contrasting braid or ribbon for cushion

METHOD

Add 1 cm seams throughout. On pattern pieces 1 and 5 add 5 cm for hem. See the Pull Out Pattern Sheet for the pattern pieces.

1 Locate, draw up and cut out the following pattern pieces from your fabric: skirt section 1; seat and front backrest 2; armrest 3; magazine pocket 4; back (includes back skirt) 5.

2 Place two pocket pieces, right sides facing, edges matching. Stitch long sides· and across one short end. Turn, press. Topstitch short end. Repeat for other pocket pieces.

3 Fold pocket so that the topstitched foldline (top of pocket) lies 3 cm below the raw edge at the other end of the pocket. Topstitch both sides with a double row of stitches for strength.

4 Pin pockets at markings on side sections of skirt piece 1. Stitch in place.

5 To make armrest covers: Join B to B. Sew armrests 3 to seat and front backrest 2, taking care to sew only the inside seams of both armrests at this stage. Join to D, E and F, clipping into the fabric of seat and front backrest 2 at turning points.

6 Fold in pleats at upper edge of back 5. Note that the only fabric extending beyond the pleat at edges is seam allowance.

7 Stitch top edge of seat and front backrest 2 to back 5, joining G to G. Stitch front and side piece around, joining 'A', 'AA' and 'K'.

8 Join 'H's at sides, starting at top of chair. Avoid seam distortion by not stitching over seams that cross 'H'. Finish stitching close to seam, starting again on other side. Finish lower edge with 5 cm hem.

Stencilled Director's Chair

❑ Remove the existing covers from your chair and use them to estimate the fabric for new covers. Don't forget to leave seam and hem allowances. It is sometimes possible to buy replacement covers for director's chairs, ready for decorating. Before you buy, check that they will fit.

❑ The manila card for making your stencils is generally available from stationery suppliers. You can, of course, use firm plastic sheets if you prefer.

MATERIALS

☐ sufficient fabric, such as a lightweight canvas
☐ screen printing inks
☐ stencil brushes or sponges (1 for each colour)
☐ two pieces of manila card, one 11.5 cm square for the flower motif and one 22 cm x 40 cm for the chequerboard
☐ mineral turpentine (white spirit)
☐ linseed oil
☐ craft knife or sharp blade
☐ board or sheet of glass for cutting stencil on
☐ eraser
☐ coloured pencils (as close as possible to the colours you are using)
☐ fine lead pencil

METHOD

See Pull Out Pattern Sheet at the back of the book for the stencil patterns.

1 Using the old covers as your pattern, cut new back and seat covers for the chair. Finish the edges, with overlocking, zigzag stitching or as you prefer, to prevent fraying, and mark the hem turnings. Do not sew the seams at this stage.

For the chequerboard stencil:

1 Mix mineral turpentine (white spirit) and linseed oil to 50:50 proportions. Apply fairly generously to both sides of the 22 cm x 40 cm manila card. Allow to dry. Remove excess oiliness with a soft cloth.

2 Draw a 2.5 cm squared grid on the card, leaving a 5 cm wide border all around the edge. Keep the chequerboard measurements as accurate as possible.

Cut a notch at the edges of the card where the 5 cm border lines meet the edges. These notches will be your placement guides.

3 Cut out alternate squares on the first line. Leave the second line. Cut the third line as for the first. Continue in this way until you reach the opposite border.

4 Measure 2.5 cm from each hem marking and draw a fine vertical pencil line. This will be the placement line for the edge of your stencil design.

5 Position your stencil on the fabric so that the notches are aligned along your pencil line. Using a coloured pencil in your first colour, trace around the inside of the stencil in the areas where you wish to use that colour.

6 Reposition the stencil for your second colour and repeat the above step, using the second colour pencil.

7 Position the stencil on the fabric, using the coloured lines as a guide. Paint in the first colour. Allow it to dry before stencilling with the second colour.

For the floral stencil:

1 Using the floral stencil on the pattern sheet, or your own design if you prefer, stencil the chair back panel. You can place the design any way you want, repeating the design on the chair seat also if you wish.

2 Prepare the 11.5 cm square stencil card in the same way as for the chequerboard stencil. Draw two diagonal pencil lines, connecting opposite corners of the card. This marks the centre of your stencil. Trace your design onto the centre of the card. Cut out the stencil. Using coloured pencils in the same colours as the paints you have chosen, draw around the elements of the stencil design.

3 Paint your design with a dabbing motion, completing one colour and allowing it to dry before painting with the other one.

4 When the paint is dry, iron the covers on the wrong side with a hot dry iron for about four to five minutes. This will set the inks so that they can be washed without the risk of your design disappearing.

5 Pin the hems at the marked turnings and check the fit before sewing. Stitch the seams as marked. Replace the covers on your chair.

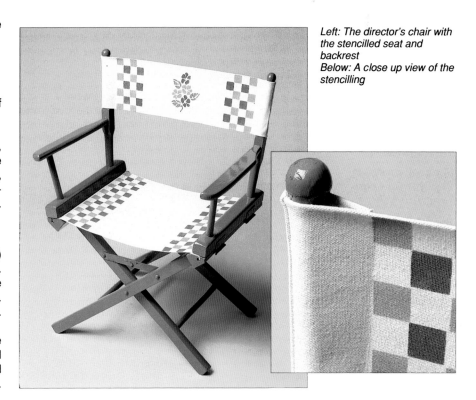

Left: The director's chair with the stencilled seat and backrest
Below: A close up view of the stencilling

Heirloom Cushions

Scatter cushions are a great way to add that finishing touch to your home and they are simple and inexpensive to make. Be as adventurous as you like in your choice of fabrics and colours. Mix and match your colours and patterns for a bright, cheerful look or keep to the one basic colour for a more subdued effect. Remember that your cushions don't all have to be the same size. Try a couple of extra large, soft ones for the corners of the sofa and some smaller ones for the armchairs.

These cushions could well become the heirlooms of tomorrow. Based on the·same pattern, they are all made from a simple calico or muslin base and then lavishly trimmed with lengths of laces, ribbons and lace motifs.

Before You Begin

❑ Cushion fronts and ruffles are trimmed before the cushion is assembled.

MATERIALS

For cushions A, B, D and E:
- ❑ fabric for one cushion front 40 cm x 40 cm, two cushion backs each 40 cm x 22 cm
- ❑ 40 cm square cushion insert
- ❑ one 30 cm zipper
- ❑ strips of fabric 22 cm wide joined to make a 3.20 m long ruffle

For cushion C:
- ❑ strip of calico 12 cm x 192 cm to be cut into sixteen 12 cm squares for cushion front, two pieces of calico, each 40 cm x 22 cm for cushion backs
- ❑ 30 cm zipper
- ❑ 40 cm square cushion insert

TRIMMING

For cushion A:
- ❑ 5.60 m of 4 cm wide crocheted cotton lace

For cushion B:
- ❑ 4.10 m of 1 cm wide patterned satin ribbon
- ❑ 2.20 m of 6 cm wide embroidered cotton braid

For cushion C:
- ❑ 2 m of 5 cm wide double-edged lace

For cushion D:
- ❑ 3.20 m of 2 cm wide crocheted cotton lace
- ❑ one 35 cm square lace centrepiece or doily

For cushion E:
- ❑ 5.30 m of 1 cm wide patterned, satin ribbon
- ❑ 6 m of 3 cm wide scalloped, crocheted cotton lace

BASIC SEWING METHOD

Apply the lace and trimmings as shown. 1 cm seams allowed throughout.

To make the basic cushion:
1 cm seams allowed throughout.

1 Place two 40 cm edges of the back pieces together with right sides facing. Stitch a 2 cm long seam at each end, leaving an opening for the zipper. Insert the zipper. Open the zipper to allow for turning the cushion.

2 Join the short ends of the ruffle strip to form a circle. Divide the circle into four equal parts, mark these quarter points. Fold ruffle strip over double, with wrong sides facing. Press.

3 Stitch a row of gathering along the raw edges. With right sides of ruffle and cushion front facing and raw edges matching, position quarter points at each corner of cushion front. Draw up the gathering to fit the side edges. Stitch in place just outside the gathering.

4 Place the cushion back and trimmed cushion front together with right sides facing. Stitch around all four sides, following the previous stitching. Turn cushion right side out.

For trimming
For cushions A, B, D and E:
Apply the trimmings as shown on the photographed cushions.

For cushion C:
1 Stitch both sides of the lace down the centre of the fabric strip then cut the strip into sixteen 12 cm squares.

2 Sew the squares together, in four rows of four squares each, noting that the direction of the lace is alternately horizontal and vertical. Sew the four rows together to form the front of the cushion.

3 Continue as for the BASIC SEWING METHOD.

B

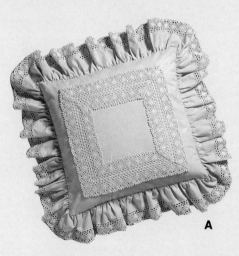

A

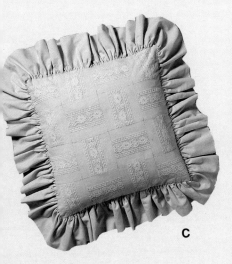

C

D

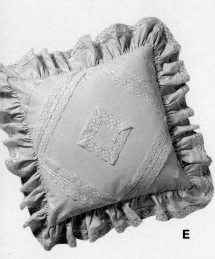

E

Dining Chairs

Very often the seat padding on dining chairs is quite sound, only needing a cover of new fabric to be reborn. These step-by-step instructions and photographs show you how to transform your dining chairs.

Before You Begin

❏ Ensure that your chair frames and padding are in good condition. It does not make much sense to spend time and money recovering the seat of a chair that's on its last legs – literally!

❏ Measure the seat of your chair to establish how much new fabric you will need for each seat. Don't forget to allow for the height of the cushioning. Use the old cover as a pattern for the new one. The lining fabric only needs to be sufficient to cover the underside of the chair base.

MATERIALS

☐ sufficient fabric and lining
☐ staple gun or upholstery tacks and a small hammer

METHOD

Allow 1.5 cm all around for turning.

1 Remove the old fabric and lining from your chair seat. Using the tip of a screwdriver or some pliers, lift out any remaining tacks or staples.

2 Using the old cover and lining as patterns, cut out your new ones.

3 Place the new cover over the seat, folding in the corners and fastening the fabric underneath the seat with a staple gun or upholstery tacks.

4 Turn in edges of lining piece. Position it in the centre of the underside of the seat so that the previous stapling is covered. Secure the lining to the frame with a staple gun or upholstery tacks.

the nicest
Napery

They say that one of the pleasures of eating good food lies in the enjoyment of the eye as well as the appetite. A lovely setting of table linen will put the finishing touch to your meal – as well as your dining room decor!

Choose a colour and style that complements your china and your dining room or kitchen colour scheme.

Stencilled Cloth and Napkins

Before You Begin

❏ Measure your table to decide on the size of your cloth by running a tape measure across the table and over the sides to the depth you wish for the overhang. Be sure to include in your fabric allowance, the tabletop measurement and overhang for all four sides. Sometimes fabric can be so wide that you do not have to join pieces to reach the required size. If this width is not obtainable, join strips so that the seams run along near the table edges, rather than one seam down the middle of the table.

❏ It is best to choose a one hundred per cent cotton fabric with a smooth finish for a tablecloth and napkins. Cotton launders well and is pleasant to handle. If you prefer the wearing qualities of man-made fibres, try using a polyester/cotton mixture.

❏ There are many ways to locate the stencil design on your tablecloth, depending on the size of the cloth and the design, and your own preference. You could place the design at each place setting, as a continuous border around the edge of the cloth or positioned to sit in from the edge of the table, as in the one shown. Bear in mind when positioning your design, that the edge of the tablecloth is not likely to be visible when you are seated at the table so much of the effect could be lost.

MATERIALS

For the tablecloth:
☐ Allow sufficient fabric to cover table top and desired overhang, plus 5 cm all around for hem

For each napkin:
☐ 60 cm square of fabric

For both:
☐ matching sewing thread
☐ manila card for the stencil
☐ mineral turpentine (white spirit)
☐ linseed oil
☐ lead pencil
☐ sharp craft knife
☐ board for cutting stencil
☐ stencilling paints
☐ stencilling brushes
☐ masking tape

METHOD

1 cm seams allowed throughout.

For the tablecloth and napkins:

1 Fold the fabric as shown in the diagram above, having the edge 'A' measure 8 cm and the hems all 1 cm.

2 Stitch across the corners, trim seams. Turn the border to the right side.

3 Pin and baste inner edge in place. Stitch down and press.

For the stencilling:

1 Mix mineral turpentine (white spirit) and linseed oil in a ratio of 50:50. Coat both sides of the manila card quite liberally with the mixture. Any excess oiliness can be wiped off with a soft cloth.

2 Draw the design onto the card. Cut out the stencil with a sharp craft knife.

3 Position the stencil on the cloth and napkins. Paint in first one colour and then any other colours one by one. Cover with masking tape any area that you wish to paint a different colour.

4 To set the colours, press on the wrong side of the fabric with a dry iron on a setting suitable for the fabric.

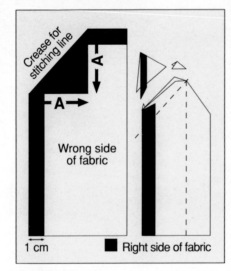

Right: The linen cloth and napkins stencilled to match the china pattern

Primary Brights

If you can sew straight, these place mats and napkins are just right for you. The skills involved are as simple as can be, and you will be delighted with the imaginative colour combinations possible. You could choose your own colours and even patterns to mix and match – black and white, pattern and plain, or simply crisscross the base with pretty braid.

Before You Begin

❏ One hundred per cent cotton fabric is ideal for making table linen. It washes well and is available in a wonderful array of colours. If you prefer a synthetic fabric for its wearing qualities, choose a cotton and polyester mixture for the best of both worlds.

Place mat with coloured bands

MATERIALS

For each place mat:

☐ piece of fabric 50 cm x 34 cm for the base
☐ polyester wadding 50 cm x 34 cm for the base
☐ piece of fabric for the contrast backing 56 cm x 40 cm
☐ five strips of contrast fabric each 34 cm x 4 cm
☐ three strips of contrast fabric each 50 cm x 4 cm
☐ matching sewing threads

METHOD

1 cm seams allowed throughout.

1 Baste fabric base to wadding around the edges and through the centre to hold the fabric smoothly in place.

2 Fold in 6 mm on the long edges of each contrast fabric strip. Press. Using dressmaker's chalk, divide the base into 6 cm squares separated by 2 cm wide contrast bands and a 2 cm wide contrast border all around. Pin bands into place on base, weaving them over and under each other as shown. Stitch along both edges of each strip to secure in place.

3 Place trimmed base onto the centre of the contrast backing piece with wrong sides facing. Baste together around the edge of the trimmed base. Note that the backing piece extends 3 cm beyond the trimmed piece on all sides. This extension will form the contrast border. Turn in 1 cm on all edges of backing piece. Mitre the contrast backing corners as shown on page 56, having A measure 4 cm.

4 Fold extensions of the backing to the right side, enclosing the edges of trimmed piece. Stitch around the inner edge of the border, close to the fold and through all thicknesses.

From left to right: Bound napkin; quilted and bound place mat; bound napkin; place mats with coloured bands and matching napkins

Napkins with contrast borders

MATERIALS

For each napkin:
- ☐ 50 cm square of main fabric
- ☐ four 50 cm x 7 cm contrast fabric strips for borders
- ☐ matching sewing thread

METHOD

1 cm seams allowed throughout.

1 Cut the ends of the fabric strips to perfect diagonals. Fold in 1 cm on the inner (shorter) edge. Press.

2 Seam the strips together at the corners to form an open square. Press the seams open.

3 Place the right side of the contrast border square over wrong side of the main fabric piece, with raw edges matching. Stitch all around the outer edge. Trim the corners to reduce bulk. Turn the border to the right side and press. Stitch around the inner edge of border, through all thicknesses.

Fig. 1

Quilted and bound place mat

MATERIALS

- ☐ two pieces of main fabric, each 50 cm x 34 cm
- ☐ polyester wadding 50 cm x 34 cm
- ☐ 1.80 m of 4.2 cm wide bias binding, either purchased or cut from a contrast fabric
- ☐ matching sewing thread

METHOD

1 cm seams allowed throughout.

1 Place the wadding between the two main fabric pieces, so that the fabrics are right side out. Baste around the edges. Using a kitchen saucer as a guide, round off the corners.

2 Using the photograph as a guide, divide the place mat into squares and mark with dressmaker's chalk. Stitch along the chalk rows to quilt.

3 Position the bias on the wrong side of the place mat, with right sides facing and with your stitching line 1 cm in from the bias binding edge and 1.5 cm from the place mat edge. Stitch bias binding around the place mat, easing it around the curved corners and tucking the raw end under at the overlap. Press under 1 cm on the other raw end of the bias binding. Fold bias binding to the right side of the place mat. Pin then stitch along the folded edge. (See Fig. 1)

Bound napkin

MATERIALS

- ☐ 50 cm square of main fabric
- ☐ 1.10 m of 4.2 cm wide bias binding, purchased or cut from contrast fabric

METHOD

1 Using a kitchen saucer as a guide, round off the corners of the napkin.

2 Bind the edges of the napkin following the directions for binding the place mat and using the diagram in Fig. 1.

Pretty Pastels

Create your own heirlooms! These place mats and napkins are sewn from lightweight pure linen – a timeless fabric that lasts and lasts.

Before You Begin

❏ All place mats and napkins, except B, are the same size and made in the same way. They differ only in the manner of trimming. The place mat and napkin B are trimmed first, then made following the BASIC SEWING METHOD.

MATERIALS

For each set:
☐ piece of fabric 60 cm x 40 cm for the basic place mat
☐ piece 60 cm x 60 cm for basic napkin

For set A:
☐ embroidery thread

For set B:
☐ six different coloured sewing threads

For set C:
☐ a motif from a floral, cotton fabric
☐ matching sewing thread

For set D:
☐ silk braid or embroidery floss, suitable for hand-stitched couching
☐ matching sewing thread

For set E:
☐ embroidery floss in the appropriate colours for your design

BASIC SEWING METHOD
1 cm seams allowed throughout.

1 Mitre corners as shown on page 56, having A measure 7 cm.

2 Fold the fabric as shown on page 56, pressing in hems and stitching lines. Stitch across corners, trim seam, turn to the right side. Press.

3 Stitch around inner folded edge. Press carefully using a warm iron and damp cloth or ironing spray.

For trimming set A:
See the Pull Out Pattern Sheet at the back of the book for the placemat and napkin embroidery design.

1 Trace the design onto one corner of the mat and napkin. Embroider the outline using embroidery floss in your chosen colours and buttonhole stitch.

2 When the embroidery is complete, carefully cut away the fabric inside the embroidered outline using small sharp scissors.

For trimming Set B:
1 Press a crease 5 cm in from all edges on both the place mat and the napkin. Using this crease as your starting and finishing point, stitch 6 rows of twin-needle stitching across the mat and napkin using six different colours. (See below.) Be sure to stitch your corners so that the stitching remains on the right side.

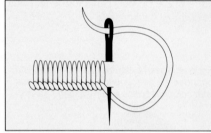

Fig. 1: Buttonhole stitching

C

B

D

2 When the stitching is complete, finish corners and borders following the BASIC SEWING METHOD on the page 60.

For set C:
1 Cut out a floral motif from a print fabric, allowing 6 mm fabric excess around motif.

2 Position appliqué pieces on the placemat and napkin. Baste. Stitch around the edge of each piece, 6 mm from the edge using a small zigzag stitch. Cut away the excess fabric, close to the stitching. Adjust your sewing machine stitch to a wider satin stitch. Stitch again over the previous stitching, enclosing raw edge as you stitch. Do this for each appliqué piece, using matching sewing thread.

For set D:
1 The couching design is worked at random onto the place mat and napkin, forming a border around the centre. If you are using a sewing machine with a braiding foot attachment, follow the manufacturer's instructions for its use. If stitching by hand, use small, evenly spaced stitches. You may like to use a metallic embroidery thread for stitching.

2 Lay the silk braid along the fabric, forming the curled design and stitch over it, securing it to the fabric. (See below)

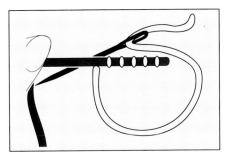

Fig. 2: Couching

For set E:
See the Pull Out Pattern Sheet at the back of the book for the pansy design.

1 Trace the pansy design from the pattern sheet onto the fabric using dressmaker's tracing paper.

2 Embroider the design as shown using long and short stitch (See Fig. 3) for the pansy petals and leaves and satin stitch for the centre of each flower as shown. (See Fig. 4)

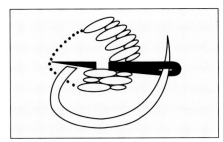

Fig. 3: Long and short stitch

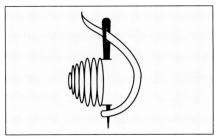

Fig. 4: Satin stitch

From left to right: Place mat and napkin sets – Set C; set B; set D; set A; set E

Fabric Know-How

Whether it's inexpensive cotton used extravagantly, patchwork quilts, lush silk drapes or antique tapestries born again as small cushions, fabrics make a statement about you and generally set the decorating theme.

You don't have to spend a lot of money – often it's the creative use of inexpensive fabrics that is the most effective. Remember, whether you're considering furniture or fabrics, good design doesn't have to cost any more than poor design.

The great variety of fabrics available to choose from can be daunting to the fledgling home decorator. Apart from traditional knowledge about fabrics and their properties, manufacturers today often have helpful information printed on the sample cards, telling you of a fabric's washing abilities and its potential for fading. They will refer to the 'wearability' of the fabric – or in other words, how strong it is! Pay attention to this valuable information. Fabrics are only guaranteed by the manufacturer if used in recommended situations.

The four natural fibres, cotton, wool, silk and linen are all familiar in home furnishing. Cotton has long been the leader for sheets, towels and most curtains. It's mass produced and this helps to make it inexpensive to manufacture into fabrics of many weights and textures. Wool is the basis of traditional and modern floor coverings. Wool is the best fabric insulator while being hard wearing, flame retardant, light and fairly waterproof. It is long-

lasting, but take care with laundering. Silk has the glamour role, providing traditional fabrics for upholstery, tassels and braids, cushions and luxury rugs. Silk is a very fine and strong fibre, a good insulator, quite expensive compared to other natural fibres, and is the most lustrous fibre of all. Linen is the world's oldest domestic fibre. Sheets and household napery have always been made from linen, with its main appeal being its sheer endurance – it never seems to wear out!

Today you still have the choice of natural fibres, but also have access to the wide range of man-made or synthetic fibres. The most commonly used of these fibres are polyester, acrylic and viscose – all produced by chemical processes and all with valuable qualities.

Synthetic fibres are often blended with man-made fibres in fabrics. This serves two purposes – the cost is reduced, and very often the synthetic fibres give added strength. Synthetic fabrics usually wash very well, the fibres do not absorb dirt and moisture, and are long wearing. They also provide insulation and effective light control.

Four Golden rules for choosing fabrics

1 Be certain that the fabric chosen is suitable for the use you intend to give it. For example, don't expect a shiny chintz to be long-wearing in a child's bedroom or lace curtains to cut out the light. Sounds sensible doesn't it? However emotions sometimes have a habit of blunting our judgement when we see

beautiful fabrics – so be warned! Always ensure you are using a fabric in a way that the manufacturer intended.

2 Be sure it is an economically sound purchase. Don't spend loads of money on areas that don't warrant the expense, but do invest in good quality fabrics for high-traffic areas or for pieces of classic design. If you simply cannot stop yourself coveting a very expensive fabric which your budget won't allow, compromise a little. Make a lining curtain for insulation and privacy and wait for the time when you can afford to purchase the fabric you have your heart set on. When that time comes you can hang your beautiful new curtains over the existing lining. Compromise on another fabric is rarely satisfying. You will always wish you had waited for the fabric you really wanted and not settled for second best.

3 If you are going to sew soft furnishings, be sure that your machine is capable of sewing your chosen fabric. Some heavily-textured fabrics and those that are light and slippery can be difficult to sew on a domestic machine.

4 Look into how you plan to care for the particular fabric and make sure the one you have chosen is suitable for this regime. For example, if you are going to wash your curtains at home rather than have them professionally cleaned, be sure that the fabric you have chosen is washable and will not shrink or distort.

A Country Kitchen

Traditionally, a country kitchen shines with the warm patina of polished timbers, slate or tile floors and an abundance of those small 'country' touches. These include wreaths of dried flowers; bowls of fruit and vegetables; collections of old china or cooking implements displayed on open shelves or in an old dresser, and a pot holder, curtains, place mats and so on, made from a pretty, small-print fabric.

You may not be in a position to scrap your existing kitchen and start again but you can add those clever details that will give your kitchen decor a country feel. Try your hand at the old craft of paper pricking and then apply it to your kitchen shelves. Sew our collection of fabric bits and pieces and don't forget the matching curtains. If your kitchen has suitable walls, adding an old-fashioned stencil border, such as the one on page 30, is a great finishing touch.

Pierced or Pricked Paper

This is one of the simplest crafts around and you don't need any glues, paints or special tools. You can use many types of paper, for example, writing papers, shelf trims, gift wrapping and even old greeting cards.

Before You Begin

❑ Use a firm type of paper but one that is not too rigid as the indentations will be hard to make.

❑ This technique is also good for trimming writing paper. Large holes can sometimes be attractive in amongst a design, and these are created with the single hole paper punch.

MATERIALS

☐ suitable paper
☐ a sharp darning needle or a noticeboard pin which has a portion of plastic at its base, for making the holes
☐ a sheet of soft particle board for resting the paper on
☐ dressmaker's pins to hold the paper and design sheet in place on the particle board
☐ a single hole paper punch used to make the larger holes
☐ a pattern design to use as a pattern

METHOD

1 Place the paper onto the particle board. Position the decorative pattern over the paper. Secure the two layers together by pinning through the design in several places so that the hole you make becomes part of the design.

2 Continue to pierce the paper, following the pattern. Make the indentations about 3 mm apart, and try to keep them evenly spaced.

Above: Pricked paper shelf edging
Left: A country kitchen with all the trimmings
Below: Pricking diagram for the shelf edging

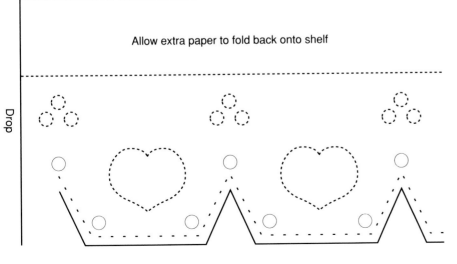

Allow extra paper to fold back onto shelf

Drop

Decorative shelf papers

Before You Begin

❑ You will need firm paper of a size which covers the shelf and allows the desired drop over the front of the shelf.

❑ You will have both raised 'bumps' and a flat surface resulting from the paper being pierced. Decide which side you wish to have as your right side. If you wish to have a combination of both you will need to flip the paper over and re-position the pattern while you work.

METHOD

1 Place the design to be pierced just in from the edge of the paper, then continue, following the general instructions for paper pricking on this page.

2 Cut the paper away to within 5-6 mm of the outside edge of the design to give the shelf paper an interesting edge.

Quilted Kitchen Set

You will see that all of these pieces use pre-quilted fabric, teamed with the matching unquilted material, or you can quilt your own fabric. To do this, baste a piece of polyester wadding to the wrong side of your plain fabric and stitch over it with a pattern of diagonal rows of stitches.

Pot holder

MATERIALS

☐ two pieces of pre-quilted cotton main fabric, each 90 cm x 20 cm or plain fabric and polyester wadding in the same size
☐ two pieces 23 cm x 20 cm main fabric and two pieces of the same size from a contrasting cotton fabric for hand pieces
☐ 3 m of corded piping
☐ matching sewing thread

METHOD

1 cm seams allowed throughout.

1 Quilt fabric, if necessary, following the instructions on How To Quilt Fabric in the box on page 67.

2 Sew corded piping to one 20 cm edge of each main fabric hand piece, with right sides facing and raw edges matching. Pin lining hand pieces over trimmed pieces, with right sides facing and raw edges matching. Stitch the 20 cm seam following previous stitching. Turn the hand pieces right sides out and press.

3 Place the trimmed hand pieces at opposite ends of one main piece, with raw edges matching. Pin in place, then place remaining main piece on top of pinned main piece, so that raw edges are matching. Pin through all thicknesses. Using a kitchen cup as a guide, round off the corners of the pot holder. Remove untrimmed main piece.

4 Pin corded piping around all the edges on the right side of the trimmed main piece, clipping the seam allowance of the piping where needed. Overlap the ends. Pull a little cord out of the piping and cut it off to eliminate bulk. Stitch around piping.

5 Place remaining main piece over trimmed piece, with right sides facing and raw edges matching. Stitch, following the previous stitching, leaving an opening for turning. Clip seams. Turn pot holder to right side and press. Handsew opening closed.

Left: Pretty and practical, this quilted pot holder is an essential in any country kitchen. Remember to use a crisp, cotton fabric in a traditional small print and to trim it with contrasting binding

Tea cosy

☐ Measure your teapot to be sure that our tea cosy will fit. Adjust the size if necessary.

MATERIALS

☐ two pieces of pre-quilted cotton main fabric and two pieces of lining fabric each 37 cm x 28 cm or plain fabric and polyester wadding in the same size
☐ 1.80 m of corded piping
☐ matching sewing thread

METHOD

1 cm seams allowed throughout.

1 Quilt fabric if necessary following instructions on HOW TO QUILT FABRIC in the box on page 67.

2 Using a kitchen cup as a guide, round off the two top corners of each main and lining fabric piece. Pin corded piping around the edge of the right side of one main fabric piece with raw edges matching and right sides facing. Stitch piping in place. Clip seam allowance of piping where necessary, for ease.

3 Place remaining main fabric piece over the trimmed piece, with raw edges matching and right sides facing. Stitch, following the previous stitching.

4 Pin piping around the bottom of the right side of the main piece, with raw edges matching and ends overlapping. Pull out a little of the cord from the piping and cut it away to eliminate bulk. Stitch piping in place. Do not turn the piece to the right side.

5 With right sides facing and raw edges matching, stitch lining pieces together around the sides and top edge. Do not turn lining to the right side. Place lower edges of the main piece and the lining together, with right sides facing and raw edges matching. Be sure to align the side seams. Stitch around the lower edge, following the previous stitching, leaving an opening for turning. Turn the tea cosy to the right side through the opening. Handsew opening closed. Push the lining up into the main piece. Attach lining to the main fabric along the seamline with invisible hand stitches.

Table napkin

MATERIALS

- [ ] one 50 cm square each of main cotton fabric and of contrasting cotton fabric
- [ ] 2.10 m of corded piping
- [ ] matching sewing thread
- [ ] 50 cm of bias binding in the same colour as the corded piping for the napkin tie

METHOD

1 Using a kitchen cup as a guide, round off the corners of the main and contrast fabric pieces.

2 Make the napkin in the same way as the place mat, omitting the quilting.

3 Fold the bias binding over double lengthways, with wrong sides facing and the folded edges matching. Stitch along folded edges. Knot the ends. Stitch the centre of the bias binding 12.5 cm down from one corner.

4 Fold the side with the tie attached in half, with wrong sides facing. Roll the opposite side of the napkin towards the end with the tie. Wrap the tie around the rolled napkin and tie into a bow.

Place mat

MATERIALS

- [ ] one piece of pre-quilted main fabric 50 cm x 34 cm or plain fabric and polyester wadding in the same size
- [ ] one piece of backing fabric in the main fabric or a contrasting one, 50 cm x 34 cm
- [ ] 1.80 m of corded piping
- [ ] matching sewing thread

METHOD

1 Quilt fabric if necessary following instructions on How To Quilt Fabric in the box on this page.

2 Using a kitchen cup as a guide, round off the corners of the main and backing fabric pieces. With right sides facing and raw edges matching, pin piping around

Above: Carry through your country kitchen decorating scheme into this matched set of quilted tea cosy, place mat and napkin. You can choose to use the same fabric as your curtains, as we have done, or you can complement your curtains with another small print in toning colours

quilted main piece, clipping the seam allowance at curves for ease. Overlap the ends of the piping. Draw out a little cord from the piping and cut it off to eliminate bulk. Stitch piping in place.

3 Place the backing piece over the main piece, with edges matching and the right sides facing. Stitch around the edge, following the previous stitching line and leaving an opening for turning the place mat. Turn the place mat to the right side through the opening. Hand sew the opening closed with small, invisible stitches. Press place mat.

HOW TO QUILT FABRIC

You can quilt your own fabric with your sewing machine, using a quilter's guide to plan the squares and spaces. The guide looks like an arm that extends from behind the sewing machine's presser foot into the centre of the machine.

The first row of stitching is made, then the quilter's guide is adjusted to sit along this stitching. Further rows of stitching are made, each one the same distance from the previous one, as measured by the quilter's guide.

It's an easy way to achieve professional-looking quilting and you can still use ornate machine stitches or twin-needle stitches for your quilting.

Bathroom Beauties

The bathroom most often shows the passage of time. The colour scheme is often not to your liking and clashes with your towels. The tiles are faded and the paintwork peeling. Don't despair! You can give your bathroom a facelift for relatively little cost.

Shower curtain

This shower curtain is totally decorative, covering a purely functional, plastic shower curtain already in place.

MATERIALS

- ☐ sufficient fabric to cover the existing curtain. Plastic curtains are not hemmed at sides and lower edge, so be sure to allow extra fabric for 5 cm deep side and lower hems, and the 10 cm turnover at the top. If necessary, join fabric lengths together with flat seams to achieve the desired size.
- ☐ matching sewing thread

METHOD

1 Fold in 1 cm on the sides, then fold another 4 cm. Press and stitch. Fold up the lower hem and stitch in the same way. Fold over 5 cm at the top then fold another 5 cm. Stitch along the first fold.

2 Make buttonholes for the curtain rings at the same intervals as they are on the plastic shower curtain. Hang the fabric curtain on the outside of the plastic one by pushing the hooks through the button-holes of both curtains at once.

3 If you wish to hook the fabric curtain out of the way or tie it to one side, you can purchase a suitable water resistant cord and tassel and attach a hook to the wall at the appropriate height.

Top right: Detail of wooden bathmat showing the threading of the cord through plastic tubing between the timber slats
Above : The prettiest bathroom showing the shower curtain, trimmed towels and wooden bathmat. The candy stripe blind is made in exactly the same way as the blind on page 14 with a frill added

Trimmed towels

A simple, but very effective decoration in the bathroom is a stack of pretty, trimmed towels on an open shelf or dresser.

Across the ends of most towels is a flat, woven band. This is the ideal place to stitch rows of ribbon or braid. You can also stitch lace or scalloped trims under the edge of a length of ribbon or fabric. Remember to trim your face cloths, bathmats and hand towels for a truly coordinated look in your bathroom.

Bath mat

This is a terrific solution to the perennial problem of soggy bathmats. An occasional scrub-down and an airing are all that are needed to keep it looking like new.

Before You Begin

❏ Decide what size bathmat you can accommodate in your bathroom before purchasing materials. Our mat measures 45 cm x 58 cm. Remember when you are measuring, that the plastic tubing makes a 2 cm gap between each piece of timber.

MATERIALS

- ☐ 10 lengths of dressed (planed) pine, each 4 cm wide x 2 cm thick x 45 cm long
- ☐ 1 m of non-perishing plastic tubing, 14 mm in diameter
- ☐ 2 m of 12 mm diameter nylon rope
- ☐ electric drill with 16 mm and 13 mm diameter drill bits
- ☐ pencil or chalk for marking

METHOD

1 Cut timber to size if necessary. Line up the lengths side by side on their 2 cm sides and rule a line 10 cm in from each end across all the timber sides. Turn the timber lengths over and repeat on the other side for accurate drill positions. Mark the halfway point in the length of each piece of timber on this line.

2 Drill right through each timber piece at centre marking, using the small bit. Then drill through the same hole with the larger bit, drilling only to a depth of 1.5 cm.

3 Cut the plastic tubing into 5 cm lengths. These will be used to separate the timber pieces. Starting at one end, thread the rope through one piece of timber and then one length of plastic tubing, then the next piece of timber and another piece of plastic tubing. Work along one row of holes, out the opposite end and back through the remaining row of holes on the other side. Knot the ends of the rope securely. Hold the knots over a lighted match to fuse the ends and stop them from fraying.

New Life for Old Tiles

If your bathroom works perfectly well but you can't stand the colour of the tiles – you have a problem. Re-tiling is costly, so some camouflage is necessary. You may of course choose wallpaper that is complimentary – so that the choice of tiles looks quite deliberate. If wallpaper does not appeal, read on for three other clever solutions.

Painting tiles

It is possible to paint tiles as you would a wall, if you prepare the surface carefully. First wash down the tiles with sugar soap or white spirit to totally remove all traces of soap scum. When the tiles are clean and dry, apply a sealer coat of a paint-on waterproofing material, such as a Bond Crete or Uni-Bond, if you can obtain it. This provides a surface to which paint will cling. Paint over the sealer coat with your chosen colour of vinyl gloss, painting over the grouting as well. You can add a stencilled border around the top of the tiles.

Etching a pattern

Make or purchase a stencil of your choice. You could use one from the Pull Out Pattern Sheet at the back of this book. Position the stencil and draw around the outlines using a chinagraph pencil which will draw on shiny surfaces. Using a small paintbrush, fill in the outlines of the design with acid etching paste,

available from hardware, stained glass or sheet glass suppliers. Allow it to dry for at least two hours. Wash off the dried paste with water. What remains is a shadowy outline of the design. This is a very subtle effect.

Etching and painting a pattern

Once you have etched the design as instructed in ETCH-ING A PATTERN, you can paint over the etched area with cold ceramic paints, from art supply stores. These paints take many hours to dry – or cure – and it will be at least two or three weeks before they are thoroughly cured. They are touch-dry in an hour or so, but take care to avoid scratching the design until it is fully cured. You can use the bathroom in the meantime, but the drying process may be prolonged by the resulting dampness. If you do not etch first, draw on the design using a chinagraph pencil and fill in with cold ceramic paints. Regardless of whether you etch first, seal the entire painted area with ceramic sealer, available from hardware stores, after the paint is dry.

Bedtime
stories

In days past, bedrooms were often the forgotten rooms in the house, at least as far as decorating was concerned – but no more! These days the decor of most bedrooms revolves around the wonderful array of bed linens available. You can dress up the most uninspiring room with clever use of fabric for sheets, pillowcases and quilt. And don't forget to carry the theme through into curtains or blinds to match.

Making your own bed linen is easy, lets you create your own decorating scheme and can save you money too! Remember to measure the bed carefully – small differences won't matter for flat sheets, but accuracy is important for ruffles or valances.

Laura Ashley (Australia) Pty Limited

Stencilled Bedhead, Cushions and Quilt

You don't need to be rich or an artist to own this original work of art! Add a little ingenuity and some stylish paintwork and you can make this bedhead yourself! The bedhead is actually an old picture frame, surrounding a stencilled fabric panel which matches the stencilled quilt. These long narrow frames were commonly available during the l920s and are usually solidly constructed of lightly carved wood. If a similar frame fails to materialise during your junk shop rambles, or your garage or attic hasn't been hiding one for years, you could make a similar frame for yourself. The moulded timber pieces are usually available at specialist timber shops, or perhaps a professional picture framer could advise you. Two identical smaller frames could also be effective, each one containing a single, smaller stencil. Place the smaller frames side by side to take up similar space to the larger frame.

As to which design you stencil, that's entirely up to you. There are a number of designs on the Pull Out Pattern Sheet at the back of this book that will all work well. Alternatively, you can purchase a variety of prepared stencils or make your own from any design or pattern that pleases you.

Bedhead

MATERIALS

- [ ] one large rectangular, wooden frame in good condition
- [ ] sufficient cotton fabric to fit into the frame, allowing approximately 10 cm around all the edges for fastening to the frame
- [ ] manila card for the stencil
- [ ] mineral turpentine (white spirit)
- [ ] linseed oil
- [ ] coloured pencils
- [ ] sharp craft knife
- [ ] board for cutting stencil on
- [ ] stencilling paints and brushes
- [ ] a staple gun or strong sewing needle and thread
- [ ] piece of firm backing board and thick polyester wadding, each the size of the inside measurement of the frame
- [ ] 3 cm wide masking tape
- [ ] wide, thick brown paper
- [ ] 2 eye hooks and wire for hanging the frame
- [ ] small tacks and a hammer

METHOD

See Page 75 for the large stencil and the Pull Out Pattern Sheet at the back of the book for the small one.

For the stencilled fabric:
Following directions on page 73, stencil the design onto the fabric so that the motifs sit evenly within the frame. Allow it to dry thoroughly. Press on the wrong side.

For making the frame:

1 Press in and sew a 1 cm hem all around fabric.

2 Place the wadding over the backing board. You may need to tape it into place temporarily. Place the stencilled fabric over wadding, positioning it so that the design is in its right position. Tape the fabric edges to the wrong side of the board, checking that you have not distorted the fabric. Staple the fabric edges to the backing board, or stitch the edges together from top to bottom and then from side to side, using a handsewing needle and strong thread. Pull the thread firmly to keep the fabric in place.

3 Place the covered board into the frame, hammering in small tacks on the back around the frame's inner edge to keep the covered board in place.

4 Cover the back of the board with brown paper, folded or cut to size. Cover the edges of the paper with masking tape, taking the tape onto the back of the frame as well. Insert the eye hooks into each side of the frame at the back. Check the required length for the hanging wire. Wind the ends of the wire securely around the eye hooks. Hang the frame at a suitable height above the bed.

Quilt cover

Before You Begin

❏ This quilt cover is designed for a single bed. The same method can be used to make a larger cover simply by increasing the number of stencilled panels used.

MATERIALS

For the quilt cover:
- ☐ 7.5 m of 90 cm wide calico or 4 m of 137 cm wide calico
- ☐ 5.5 m of 112 cm wide homespun cotton in a contrasting colour to match or complement your chosen stencil colour.
- ☐ 60 cm of continuous zipper or two 30 cm dress zippers
- ☐ manila card for making the stencil
- ☐ craft knife or sharp, pointed blade
- ☐ stencil brushes or sponges, one for each colour
- ☐ cutting board for cutting stencil on
- ☐ linseed oil
- ☐ mineral turpentine (white spirit)
- ☐ stencilling paints

METHOD

See Pull Out Pattern Sheet at the back of the book for the floral stencil design.

For the stencilling:

1 Coat the manila card with a 50:50 mixture of mineral turpentine (white spirit) and linseed oil. Allow it to dry.

2 Trace the design onto the card and cut it out with the sharp knife. You can cut both leaf and flower designs on the one card.

3 Cut the main fabric into twelve squares each 49 cm x 49 cm. Fold each square

Stencilled cushion

MATERIALS
- ☐ one 40 cm square of main fabric to be stencilled for the front, two pieces 22 cm x 40 cm for cushion back
- ☐ 30 cm zipper
- ☐ contrast fabric strip 1.60 m x 8 cm for border
- ☐ contrast fabric strip 3.20 m x 22 cm for ruffle
- ☐ 40 cm cushion insert

METHOD

1 cm seams allowed throughout.

1 Stencil the same floral motif as on the quilt onto the cushion front, following the stencilling instructions on page 73.

2 Cut the 8 cm wide contrast strip into four 40 cm lengths, then cut each end of each strip at a perfect diagonal. Join the four strips into an open square by seaming the corners together, stopping the stitching on each corner 1 cm from the inner edge. Turn in 1 cm on the inner edges of the square, press.

3 Place the border square onto the stencilled front, with the wrong side of the square facing the right side of the cushion front and matching raw edges. Baste along inner edges of the border square, then stitch through all thicknesses.

4 Join short ends of 22 cm wide strip to form a circle. Fold the strip in half lengthways, with wrong sides together. Divide the strip into quarters and mark with pins, having the seam as one quarter point. Gather along the raw edges. Draw up the gathering. Pin the ruffle to the right side of the front, with a quarter point at each corner, right sides facing and raw edges matching. Stitch through all thicknesses just inside the gathering.

5 Join back pieces along 40 cm edge, using a 2 cm seam allowance and leaving a 30 cm opening for the zipper in the middle. Press seams open. Insert the zipper into the opening. Open the zipper.

6 Pin the back to the front with right sides facing, keeping the ruffle out of the way. Stitch around the edge. Trim the corners. Turn the cushion cover right side out through the zipper opening. Place cushion insert inside cover.

---

in half, then in half again. Mark the fold point – this is the centre of your square.

4 Place a fabric square on a flat surface, suitable for painting on. Hold it in place with pins or tape. Position your stencil on the fabric square. Paint one colour version of the design onto six squares and the other six squares with the second colour. Allow them to dry, then iron on the wrong side with a medium to hot, dry iron, to set the paint.

For the sewing:

1 cm seams allowed throughout and all pieces of the quilt are joined with right sides facing and raw edges even.

Note: Fabric strips A,B and C have been specified approximately 10 cm longer to allow for fabric movement during sewing. You may prefer to add a little more. The back of the quilt is cut out once the front is finished and can be measured accurately.

1 Cut the contrasting homespun fabric into the following strips: two pieces each 7 cm x 2.15 m for A, two pieces each 7 cm x 1.60 m for B, two pieces each 7 cm x 2.10 m for C, 9 pieces 7 cm x 49 cm for D.

2 Lay out the printed squares in three rows of four in alternating colours. Position the squares so that the stems of one colour hang 'down' the quilt and the stems of the other colour point 'up' the quilt. Starting with the first vertical row of four squares, and using three of the D strips, join the squares into a long panel,

with a D strip separating each one. Keep the layout of the squares in mind when joining the strips to the squares. Press all seams towards the strips. Repeat this procedure with the other two rows of four squares, again checking that your squares have remained according to your layout.

3 Connect the first complete long panel to the second one with one of the C strips, and then the second to the third with the other C strip.

4 Sew the B strips along the top and bottom of the quilt, then sew the A strips along both sides.

5 If necessary, recut the edges of your quilt front to make them straight. Measure the quilt front, and cut the backing piece to the same width as the front but 3 cm longer.

6 Cut across the backing strip 12 cm up from the lower edge. Rejoin these pieces in a 1.5 cm seam, leaving a 60 cm opening in the middle for the zipper or zippers. Press the seam open. Insert the zipper. If you are using two dress zippers, sew them so that the pull tabs are in the centre of the opening. When they are both pulled back, the opening will be of sufficient size to insert the quilt.

7 Place the back and front together, with right sides facing and stitch around the edges. Turn the quilt cover to the right side through the zipper opening.

This is the larger stencil outline for the pillows, bedhead and the floorcloth (page 42). See the Pull Out Pattern Sheet at the back of the book for the quilt stencil and the smaller floral stencil

Bed Linen

❏ Sheeting fabrics are most appropriate for making bed linen. Cotton dress fabrics are also ideal but you will have to sew lengths together to achieve the correct size. Use flat seams for this purpose, being sure to conceal raw edges. Sheeting fabric widths vary from 228 cm to 250 cm, from selvage to selvage. The quantities given in our charts (see Pull Out Pattern Sheet at the back of the book) relate to these widths, calculated on standard sizes of manufactured sheets and quilt covers.

❏ All our sheets and quilt covers are cut with selvages at the top and bottom while the side edges have been hemmed. However check your own bed measurements before you begin. You may have to reverse this arrangement and have the selvages on the sides and hems at the top and bottom. Dress fabrics should be joined with seams running vertically down the sheet or quilt cover so selvages will be on the sides and top and bottom are hemmed.

❏ Make your quilt cover to fit your quilt, allowing some ease. Measure your own quilt before purchasing materials. Consider using contrasting fabrics for the front and back of your quilt, making it reversible.

Quilt cover

MATERIALS

☐ sufficient fabric for your quilt, allowing for front and back
☐ some form of closure, such as a zipper or a hook and loop tape, such as Velcro. If no zipper is available that is long enough, sew in two long dress zippers, with their pulltags at the centre. When both zippers are open, the space is large enough to insert quilt
☐ matching sewing thread

METHOD

1 cm seams allowed throughout.

1 If using sheeting, place the selvages at the top and bottom edges. If using cotton craft fabrics, join lengths with flat seams, to achieve the overall size required for the front and back.

2 Place front and back pieces together with right sides facing. If you are using a zipper to close the quilt cover, join front to back at both ends of one short side using a 1.5 cm seam, leaving the correct opening for your zipper. Press seam allowance open. Insert zipper and open it.

3 Place front and back together so that right sides are facing. Sew right around the edges, using a 1.5 cm seam.

4 Turn the quilt cover to the right side through the open zipper.

Bed ruffle or valance

❏ It is difficult to give exact measurements and fabric quantities for a bed ruffle as beds are of so many different heights. The base or flat part of the ruffle is the same size as the mattress top plus seam allowances. The frill is the same depth as the height of bed base from floor, plus hem and seam allowances. It should be 4 times as long as the bed length plus 4 times the bed width.

METHOD

1 cm seams allowed throughout.

1 For beds with no bed posts or footboard, simply hem bedhead end of the base fabric piece.

2 Join frill pieces to make one continuous strip. Hem both short ends and one long edge of the frill. Gather the raw edge. Pin the gathered edge to the raw edges of the base piece with right sides together and raw edges even. Adjust gathering to fit. Stitch frill in place. Press.

3 For beds with posts, hem the head end as above. The frill will need to be made in three sections, to begin and end on either side of the posts. Each section of the frill should be twice as long as the equivalent part of the base piece. Hem the short ends. Hem one long side of each frill piece. Gather the raw edge of each piece and pin to the edges of the base piece with right sides facing and the raw edges matching. Adjust gathers to fit. Stitch.

4 To sew ties to fasten around the bed posts, sew 10 cm of elastic to one end

of each tie and the other end to the valance corner. This will take the strain off the ties and prevent the stitching from snapping.

Plain pillowcase with contrast panel

MATERIALS

☐ fabric piece 50 cm x 1.60 m
☐ contrast panel of fabric 50 cm x 15 cm
☐ 50 cm of contrast purchased bias binding or a 3 cm x 50 cm fabric strip

METHOD

1 cm seams allowed throughout.

Ruffled pillowcase

MATERIALS

☐ Cut one front pillowcase piece 78 cm x 50 cm and two pillowcase back pieces, one 70 cm x 50 cm and another 22 cm x 50 cm

☐ Cut two 5.20 m long strips (join lengths if necessary) for ruffles, one 10 cm wide from the main fabric, another 12 cm wide from contrast fabric

METHOD

1 cm seams allowed throughout.

1 Place two ruffle strips together with right sides facing and one long edge matching. Stitch along matched long edge. Press seam flat. Fold the strip over with wrong sides facing, matching remaining long raw edges. You now have a strip with a border of contrast at the folded edge.

2 Join the short ends of the strip to form a continuous circle. Gather the raw edges. Pin the ruffle around the edge of the pillowcase front piece, with right sides facing and raw edges matching. Stitch just outside the line of gathering.

3 Narrow hem one 50 cm edge of each back piece. Place both back pieces on top of the front piece, with right sides facing, overlapping the hemmed edges at the centre, and with outside edges matching. Pin and baste around the outside edge.

4 Stitch around the outside edge through all thicknesses, taking care that the frill lies flat towards the middle of the pillowcase. Turn the pillowcase to the right side and press.

1 Turn in 1 cm on the raw edge at one 50 cm end of the main fabric piece, then turn another 1 cm. Press. Stitch. Place the contrast fabric panel at the remaining 50 cm end, with the right side of the panel facing the wrong side of the pillowcase and raw edges matching. Stitch across 50 cm end. Turn panel to the right side of the pillowcase. Press under 1 cm on the remaining raw edge of the 50 cm edge of the contrast panel.

2 Fold bias strip over double with wrong sides together, press. Slide raw edge under pressed edge of contrast panel. Stitch through all thicknesses, securing contrast panel and bias strip to the pillowcase.

3 Fold pillowcase as shown in the diagram on this page, with right sides

facing. Stitch sides. Take care to secure the stitching well at the open end of the pillowcase. Turn to the right side and press.

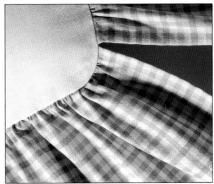

Above: Coordinated bed linen in a patchwork of fresh colours and patterns
Above left: Corner of the ruffled cushion showing the contrast binding
Above right: The corner of the bed ruffle showing the attachment of the frill and the split for bed post

To make the cuddly lamb toy, use the large outline on the Pull Out Pattern Sheet, enlarged to twice the size and cut two shapes from brushed fabric. Stitch around the edge with right sides facing, leaving an opening for stuffing. Turn to the right side. Stuff lightly with polyester wadding and outline the features as indicated using embroidery stitches.

The large, square net is edged with purchased satin blanket binding that has been stencilled to match the sheets.

Baby's Room

Decorating a room for a new baby is a true labour of love. Ideally your decor should 'grow' with the baby and still be fresh in a couple of years time. This means avoiding tiny baby motifs in fabric and looking for something a little more timeless, such as a crisp gingham or one of the appealing prints now available.

Trimmed curtains

Before You Begin

❏ See the Pull Out Pattern Sheet at the back of the book for how to measure your window and estimate fabric quantities. Quantities for trimmings will depend on the size of your curtains.

☐ Decide whether you wish to have two curtains that open in the middle and are pulled to each side, or a single curtain. If two curtains are your choice, halve the width prescribed and add an extra 5 cm to each curtain for the centre hem allowances. Sewing instructions are given for one curtain, simply make two using the same method.

MATERIALS

☐ sufficient main curtain fabric (see diagram for measuring on the Pull Out Pattern Sheet at the back of the book)
☐ three strips of contrast fabric 15 cm wide x the length of your curtains for the side panels; another piece of contrast fabric 15 cm wide x width of your main curtain plus side borders for the lower panel
☐ two strips of contrast fabric, each 15 cm x 55 cm for tie backs, one for stencilling, one for lining
☐ a piece of fusible interfacing 15 cm x 55 cm
☐ 20 cm bias binding or 3 cm wide fabric strips
☐ 2 cm diameter dowelling or a curtain pole to suit your window
☐ two support brackets and screws
☐ curtain tie back hook
☐ manila card for the stencil
☐ linseed oil
☐ mineral turpentine (white spirit)
☐ pencil
☐ sharp craft knife
☐ stencil brushes and paints
☐ cutting board

METHOD

See Pull Out Pattern Sheet at the back of the book for the lamb stencil design. 1 cm seams allowed throughout.

1 Place the two side panel pieces together with right sides facing. With a pencil, mark a perfect diagonal at one end. Cut off fabric along this line on both panels. Also mark and cut off perfect diagonals at both ends of the bottom contrast panel. Sew the contrast panels together at the diagonal seams, with right sides together and stopping the stitching 1 cm from the inner edge, to form a U shape. Press in 1 cm all around inner edge.

2 Place the contrast panels on the curtain so that the right side of the contrast panels faces the wrong side of the curtain and raw edges are matching. Pin and baste. Stitch around the outside edge.

3 Press the seam and the contrast panel to the right side of the curtain. Stitch the pressed inner edge to the curtain through all thicknesses. Press. Stencil the border now if desired.

4 Turn in 1 cm at the top, then turn another 7 cm. Press. Stitch. Stitch again 3.5 cm from the top. This row of stitching forms the pocket for inserting a rod and will have a frilled effect when the curtain is in position.

5 Install the brackets. Slide the curtain onto the pole, adjusting the gathers to fit. Hang the curtain.

Above: Stencil the curtain tie back with a lamb to match the sheets. Its features can be stencilled or embroidered and you can sew on a tiny bow as we have done

For the tie back:

1 Stencil the tie back piece following the instructions on page 73. Interface the stencilled tie back. Open out the bias binding and press flat. Fold the fabric strip or bias over double, with right sides facing and raw edges matching. Stitch the long side. Turn and press. Cut into two 10 cm pieces. Pin both ends of one length to one end of the stencilled tie back, with right sides facing and raw edges matching. Repeat for the other end with the remaining length. Place the tie back lining over the stencilled tie back. Stitch around the edges leaving an opening for turning. Turn. Press neatly.

2 Install the hook at the appropriate height. Place the tie back around the curtain and secure by hooking the loops over the hook.

Bassinet quilt

This pretty cover is one of the simplest ways of constructing a quilt that we know of! With the same technique you can make quilts of any size.

Before You Begin

☐ You will need to work out how many squares and what size squares you will need to make up a quilt to fit your bassinet. The cover shown is 5 squares wide x 63 squares long, where each square is 12 cm x 12 cm. Each 'pillow' of the quilt has a front and a back so for a quilt like this one you will need about 50 cm each of two main fabrics that are 115 cm wide.

☐ As the quilt will need to be washable, pre-shrink all fabric before sewing.

MATERIALS

☐ sufficient cotton or polycotton fabric
☐ polyester fibre for stuffing
☐ self-fabric rouleaux or contrasting ribbon

METHOD

1 cm seams allowed throughout.

1 Cut out the required number of squares from each fabric. Pair up one square from each fabric with right sides facing. Stitch around three sides leaving the remaining side open for inserting the stuffing. Clip the corners and turn the pillow right side out, making sure to push the corners out carefully. Press, turning under 1 cm on open edges.

Below: A close up of the bassinet quilt showing how the 'pillows' are joined

2 Place the pillows in rows as determined by your quilt size, butting the edges together accurately. Sew butted edges of adjoining pillows together, using a zigzag or similar stitch.

3 Stuff pillows, taking care not to place too much stuffing in each square as it will be difficult to hold the edges together while sewing. Place open edges of one row of pillows butted to the stitched edge of the next row. Stitch together, using zigzag stitch or similar stitching. Continue joining rows in this way until desired quilt size is reached.

4 Knot the ends of 25 cm lengths of rouleaux or ribbon and stitch the centre of each length securely to the points where the pillows meet. Tie rouleaux or ribbon into bows.

Sheets

These pretty sheets are trimmed with gingham and have a stencilled pattern to match the one on the curtains.

MATERIALS

For each sheet:
- ☐ 90 cm of 115 cm wide fabric
- ☐ an additional strip, of either contrast or of main fabric, 90 cm x 15 cm for the trimmed band
- ☐ 90 cm x 5 cm strip of gingham fabric
- ☐ matching sewing thread
- ☐ stencilling equipment as for the nursery curtains

METHOD

1 cm seams allowed throughout.

1 Mark the positions for the stencilled lambs across the 15 cm wide band. Stencil the band following the stencilling instructions on page 73.

2 Press under 1 cm on the lower edge of the stencilled band. Place the stencilled band on the top of the sheet so the right side of the band faces the wrong side of the sheet, having the lamb's feet closest to the edge to be stitched. Stitch along the top and side edges of the band and sheet. Turn the band to the right side. Press.

3 Fold fabric strip over double with wrong sides facing and pin under the pressed edge of the band. Stitch down through all thicknesses.

4 Hem all remaining edges of the sheet to finish. Press.

Pillow shape

MATERIALS

- ☐ 30 cm of 115 cm wide fabric to match the sheets
- ☐ a piece of quilter's polyester wadding the size of your pillow shape (see below)
- ☐ sewing thread

METHOD

1 cm seams allowed throughout.

1 Make a pattern for pillow shape by tracing the curved outline of the top of your bassinet mattress and have it measure about 30 cm long. It will look a little like a half-circle. Cut two pillow shapes from the main fabric and one from the wadding.

2 Stencil a lamb on one fabric piece, using the same method as for the sheet band and curtain tie back.

3 Place wadding against wrong side of the stencilled fabric. Baste together.

4 Place remaining piece over trimmed piece, right sides facing and raw edges matching. Stitch around edge, with an opening for turning at one side. Turn shape to right side. Press. Hand stitch closed.

Above left: Baby's bassinet with stencilled pillow shape, stencilled and trimmed sheet and pillow quilt. Make the fluffy lamb toy to cuddle

---

Acknowledgments

The publishers would like to acknowledge the generosity of the following friends:

A SELECTION OF PHOTOGRAPHS SUPPLIED BY: Laura Ashley (Australia) Pty Limited; Nairn Floors; Country Form; IKEA; Australian Wool Corporation; Dupont; Lifestyle; Forbo; Amber Tiles
CURTAIN ACCESSORIES: Curtrax, Paddington
BRAIDS AND SILK TIE-BACKS: Boyac, Rushcutters Bay
COLLECTIONS: Sue and Paul Whitter
ANAGLYPTA WALLPAPER AND FABRICS: Laura Ashley
CUSHION BRAID AND TRIMS: McCalls
RIBBONS: Offray
KITCHEN FABRICS: Liberty
ALL CRAFT FABRICS: Ray Toby Pty Ltd, NSW
FURNISHING FABRICS: John Kaldor
POTTERY ACCESSORIES: Country Floors, Willoughby NSW
CERAMIC PAINTS: Pebeo
TOWELS: Canning Vale, Australia
All craft items sewn on Bernina and Pfaff sewing machines.

Pull Out Pattern Sheet Guide

The Pull Out Pattern Sheet at the back of the book has the following information:
- ❏ Window Measurement diagram for curtains
- ❏ Cafe Curtain cut-out template
- ❏ Cord threading diagram for the Festoon Blind
- ❏ Construction diagram for the Roman Blind
- ❏ Pattern for the Director's Chair
- ❏ Placemat and Napkin embroidery designs
- ❏ Stencils for the Quilt, Floorcloth and Bedhead
- ❏ Bed Linen fabric quantities chart
- ❏ Lamb stencils for Baby's Room